Easy Vegetarian Cooking

with

Herbs and Spices

by Triset De Fonseka

Front cover photograph by Jayantha Wedasinghe, Sri Lanka
Back cover and food photography by Harry De Fonseka

Note for Librarians: A cataloguing record for this book is available from Library and Archives
Canada at www.collectionscanada.ca/amicus/index-e.html
ISBN 1-4120-7337-5

*Printed in Victoria, BC, Canada. Printed on paper with minimum 30% recycled fibre. Trafford's print shop
runs on "green energy" from solar, wind and other environmentally-friendly power sources.*

Offices in Canada, USA, Ireland and UK
This book was published *on-demand* in cooperation with Trafford Publishing. On-demand
publishing is a unique process and service of making a book available for retail sale to the
public taking advantage of on-demand manufacturing and Internet marketing. On-demand
publishing includes promotions, retail sales, manufacturing, order fulfilment, accounting and
collecting royalties on behalf of the author.

Book sales for North America and international:
Trafford Publishing, 6E–2333 Government St.,
Victoria, BC v8t 4p4 CANADA
phone 250 383 6864 (toll-free 1 888 232 4444)
fax 250 383 6804; email to orders@trafford.com
Book sales in Europe:
Trafford Publishing (uk) Limited, 9 Park End Street, 2nd Floor
Oxford, UK oxi 1hh UNITED KINGDOM
phone 44 (0)1865 722 113 (local rate 0845 230 9601)
facsimile 44 (0)1865 722 868; info.uk@trafford.com
Order online at:
trafford.com/05-2232

10 9 8 7 6 5 4

please replace with colour insesrts

This cookbook is dedicated to my Dearest Grandmother.
My culinary teacher.

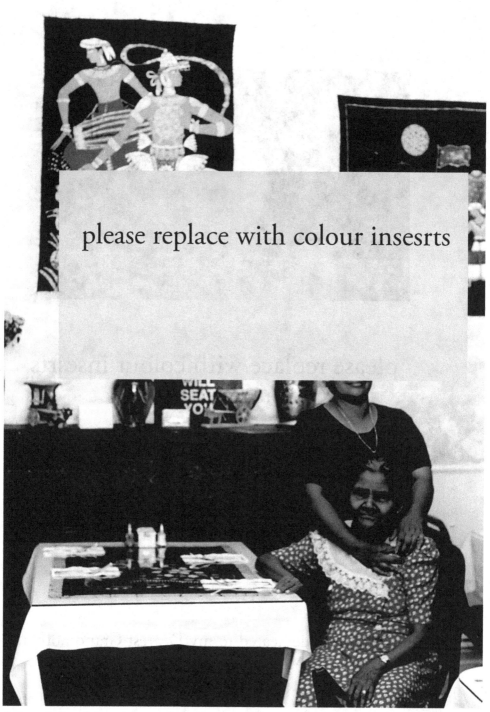

please replace with colour insesrts

Mom, God has blessed me with many gifts. But the most precious gift is your love and prayers.

Introduction

I thank GOD for his blessings of talent, knowledge and wisdom to write my second cookbook _Easy Vegetarian Cooking with Herbs and Spices_. AYUBOWAN (ahh-you-bo-wan) a Sri Lankan greeting which means blessings for a long healthy life. The recipes in my cookbook travel beyond the boundaries of traditional cooking. They are inspired by my beautiful country, Sri Lanka, a paradise rich in natural beauty with tropical forests and exotic beaches in the Indian Ocean, formerly known as Ceylon.

Continually I remind myself of my childhood memories and how I gained all my knowledge and experience from the hands and wisdom of my Grandmother whom I considered as my expert culinary teacher. I remember spending time with my Grandmother in our small kitchen, watching her cook age-old traditional healthy entrees, appetizers soups, salad_____eration to my gener_____made a mistake; she_____ous but worthwhile_____ulinary cook even th_____

In Sri L_____ to use coco_____ combined _____ spices to cre_____ curry powd_____ and gives an exotic taste and fragrance to a dish. For a healthier alternative in various recipes in my cookbook, I have recommended soymilk as a substitute to coconut milk to prepare a low fat and low cholesterol meal.

Taste is my primary concern. Most Sri Lankans dislike using scales, weights, or measures to prepare food. Recipe measures are prepared based on an individual's own judgment and taste. For example, a

please replace with colour insesrts

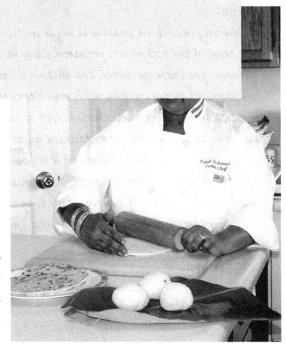

pinch of this, a generous dash of that, a sprinkling of salt or a squeeze of limejuice, all to adjust the spices and seasoning according to ones' taste. A bit of curry sauce called gravy is spooned into the palm of ones' hand to taste the balance of seasonings and flavors in a dish. Spices are ground fresh daily on a grinding stone into a paste to the type of dish or meal been prepared for the day. Sri Lankans like to shop daily for fresh bread, vegetables and fruits. Lunch is taken early in the afternoon. Rice is the staple food served in a meal with protein, legumes, vegetables and greens, thereby providing a balanced meal for lunch, to boost the immune system and in order to live a youthful healthy life.

It is traditional to have afternoon tea with cakes, cookies, sandwiches or savory pastries. The British introduced this enjoyable, relaxing tradition to the Sri Lankan People. Dinner is taken late in the evening, as it is usually served as a small light meal.

On ⟨…⟩ ries cooking in clay ⟨…⟩ ng coconut and pou ⟨…⟩ thods of Sri Lankan ⟨…⟩

The ⟨…⟩ hat capture the art ⟨…⟩ nd friends with fo ⟨…⟩ the palate. Recipes ⟨…⟩ to prepare, tasteful, ⟨…⟩ , hair, and stabilizing cholesterol and blood sugar levels.

please replace with colour insesrts

Most of the recipes are prepared daily in my restaurant, Aralia, where I use my gift of wisdom, passion, experience, and imagination to create a traditional experience. The recipes are prepared in my kitchen with much tender loving care from my heart to the table where my customers enjoy the experience of a healthy balanced and tasteful meal, and write amazing comments in my restaurant guest book. I hope you will prepare the curry powder recipe included in my cookbook or it is available for purchase at my restaurant or by mail order. Exotic vegetables are available at Asian food stores or international supermarkets. I want you to enjoy, and have an amazing experience creating my recipes in my cookbook, Easy Vegetarian cooking with Herbs and Spices!

Triset De Fonseka.

Acknowledgement

First and foremost, I thank God, my Savior, for his unconditional love, being my healer, protector, counselor, and hearing my prayers for courage to take many steps in life to fulfill my dreams in this blessed country, my home, America.

My ever-loving gratitude and thanks to my late grandmother, Claudia Francisco for being my best culinary teacher. My gratitude and thanks to my late Aunt Zena Peters for all the support received throughout my childhood years. My enduring love, gratitude and sincere thanks to my late dad, Wilfred Francisco for giving and showing unconditional love, affection, guidance, and support, while growing up until he passed away. May all of you rest in peace!

My unconditional love and sincere thanks goes thousands of miles away in Sri Lanka to my dearest mom, Bertha Francisco for her constant powerful prayers, love and support and encouragement. I miss you!

My sincere appreciation and special thanks to Mr. Chunk Martin, Cincinnati Enquirer, Rita Nader-Heikenfeld, C.C.P., Culinary Educator and Syndicated Food Columnist, and John Schaefer. It is an honor to have you all write about me, my food and restaurant, Thank You!

A special thanks to all my fans for purchasing my first and second cookbooks.

Thank you to all my loyal customers many of whom cook from my cookbooks and visit my restaurant regularly to enjoy my food and for writing excellent comments in my guest book and for their patronage. My cooking class students thank you for your enthusiasm in wanting to learn my traditional and original recipes and special cooking secrets.

To all my brothers, sisters and their families who are miles away: I love you all from the bottom of my heart!

Most of all, I thank my loving and supportive husband, Harry, my son, Ryan and my daughter, Rochelle. Thank you for the love, support, encouragement, patience, being by my side at all times and believing and having faith in me that I can do it! Thank you for helping me to make my cookbook a success!

People's Comments Regarding My First Cookbook,

Easy Vegetarian Cooking with Herbs and Spices

"Our daughter, who is a vegetarian, has to have Triset's cooking when she comes to visit. She is a walking encyclopedia for unusual dishes."   --Helen Williams.

"I have found these meals to be exceedingly tasty and delicious. I have found them to be very unusual from the kinds of cuisine that we are accustomed to in the United States. I recommend very highly her culinary expertise and would be happy to recommend her to anyone, on both the quality and presentation of her food." -- Joseph M.Gromada, M.D.

"Outstanding recipes! Good tasting, nutritious while low in calories. -- Ted Nicholas
                    Author of How to Publish a Book and Sell a million Copies

"I just wanted to let you know how much I have enjoyed your cookbook. It was a thrill for my wife, myself and my children to read and attempt to perfect some of these recipes. We are vegetarians and there are some delicious recipes within the book that are great for vegetarians and also significantly different from most vegetarian meals that we have been exposed to. Not only are the meals extremely healthy from a gastroenterological standpoint... "
                                        -- Alan V. Safdi, M.D.

"You are indeed a gifted individual who has been able to tickle many pallets with your fine selection of exotic cooking."   --Theodore E. Buka, M.D.

"We have enjoyed the incredible Sri Lankan cuisine created by Triset Defonseka for many years now and feel that her talents are abundant. We specially appreciate her ability to handle our requirements as vegetarians with such creativity and style. "
                                        -- Bruce and Carol Jodar.

"We would both give our highest praise possible to your cooking! I can't wait to try to duplicate some of your dishes from the cookbook,"   --Mair Berkley.

"Thank you for such an enjoyable afternoon of cooking instructions, good food, and fun! My family, friends, and I thoroughly enjoyed the food and out time with you"
                                        -- Jacqueline B. Dickens.

"Your book was a big hit with our customers. We are all grateful for the food brought by you- it was enjoyed by customers and staff alike! We wish you continued success."
-- Drew Gores.

"Recipes from her book, Easy Cooking with Herbs and Spices, were tested out on my friends and family with great applause. The food was delicious, interesting and different and perfect."
--Marie Lalor Brown
Associate Vice President.
Investment & Trust Specialist, A.G Edwards & Sons, Inc.

"Our customers were very receptive to the sale of your attractive cookbook, Easy Vegetarian Cooking with Herbs and Spices, during the holidays. They were dazzled by the wonderful food made from your easy to follow recipes. "   --Ann Griffith
Manager of The Red Radish Gourmet Kitchen Store.

"I have on several occasions, had the opportunity to sample the products of the culinary talent of Triset De Fonseka. Each time as proven to be a pleasant experience in that the dishes prepared were very pleasing both to the eye and the taste buds."
--Jerry Kanter
Public Accountant

"I want to congratulate on the publication of your cookbook. I have prepared and eaten several dishes as they are delicious".   --Sir John Krimm S.N. D. de N.

Contents

Appetizers

Spinach Pastries

For Filling:

1 (10-oz.) pkg. frozen spinach
½ c. feta cheese, broken up into sm. pieces
3 T. country Dijon mustard
1 sm. onion chopped
½ c. shredded mozzarella cheese

Thaw spinach in colander. Press spinach to drain water. In a bowl, combine spinach, feta cheese, mustard and onions. Mix well. Add mozzarella cheese and mix. Set aside.

For Pastries:

Flour for sprinkling
1 (17 ½-oz.) frozen puff pastry, thawed
Water for brushing

Unfold pastry sheets. On a floured surface roll out one sheet of puff pastry, sprinkle pastry sheet with a little flour and roll slightly. Turn sheet over and repeat the process. Cut into 4-inch squares (or any size you prefer). Place a little spinach mixture in middle of square. Brush edges with water. Fold in half and seal with fork. Prick top pastry with fork to allow steam to escape. Arrange pastries on cookie sheet. Repeat until all pastry sheets are used. Bake in preheated oven at 400 degrees (F) for 20 minutes or until golden brown.

Spicy Deviled Eggs With Yogurt Coriander Dip

6 hard-boiled eggs, shelled
1 ½ c. yogurt coriander dip, page 189
¼ c. red bell pepper, minced

Cut eggs in halves. Remove yolks: transfer to a bowl and set aside. Combine coriander yogurt dip with egg yolks and mix to make a paste. Pat egg whites with paper towel; fill the egg whites with mixed egg yolk and coriander paste. Sprinkle with minced bell peppers to garnish.

Pattie Dough Without Milk

(And How To Make Patties)

2 c. all-purpose flour (and more flour reserved for dusting)
¾ tsp. salt
2 T. butter-flavored shortening
1 egg yolk (reserve white for brushing)
¾ c. ice water
Vegetable oil for frying
Reserve additional flour and ice water on side if necessary
Vegetable filling, page 5

On floured surface, sift flour and salt together. Make a well; add butter and egg yolk. Mix with hands. Gradually add ice water. Knead well, adding more flour and ice water if necessary, until dough holds together to form a soft ball, which feels elastic, easy to work, and does not stick. If sticky, add more flour and knead slightly. Wrap dough in foil or waxed paper: place in refrigerator and chill for ½ hour. Cut dough into portions; dust more flour on surface. Roll out one portion with rolling pin to form a sheet; sprinkle with flour; turn sheet over and do the same. Cut 3-inch circles, or any size you prefer. Place a teaspoon of vegetable filling in each circle; brush around filling with reserved egg white. Fold in half and press, seal with fork. Sprinkle flour on baking sheet and arrange patties; continue to do the same until all dough and filling is used up. Deep fry patties in batches until golden brown. Transfer patties onto paper towels; serve with chutney or sauce.

Note:
Use fresh oil to fry patties.

Vegetable Filling For Patties

2 T. olive oil or canola oil
1 c. shallots chopped
1 c. shredded carrots
1med. potato, boiled and mashed
1 c. finely sliced leaks, white and green parts
1 tsp. vegetable curry powder, page 196
Salt, fresh pepper and limejuice to taste
¼ c. Chopped parsley

Heat nonstick skillet on medium high heat; add oil, sauté shallots and carrots. Add mashed potato and leaks sauté 2 minutes, stirring constantly. Add salt, pepper and limejuice; mix well to combine. Add parsley and mix well. Remove from heat, set aside to cool, for filling patties.

Stuffed Banana Peppers With Chickpea Dip

8 banana peppers, cut lengthwise into halves
2 c. white wine vinegar
2 c. cooked chickpeas, page 89
½ c. soy yogurt
3 shallots, minced
Juice of 2 lemons
2 T. tahini paste
4 T. olive oil
1/3 c. chopped roasted red bell pepper
¼ c. chopped parsley

Under running cold water, rinse and remove seeds from cut peppers. Arrange peppers in a square dish. Pour vinegar over, cover and refrigerate 6 to 8 hours, turning peppers occasionally to absorb vinegar. Combine chickpeas, yogurt, shallots, garlic and lemon juice in food processor, process for 1 minute. Add tahini paste and 3 tablespoons olive oil; process to a smooth paste, scraping down sides. Transfer to a bowl. Add roasted peppers with reserved 1 tablespoon olive oil and mix to combine. Set aside. Drain peppers and pat dry with paper towels. Fill peppers with chickpea dip, garnish with parsley. Arrange on flat platter to serve.

Note:
Wear rubber gloves when working with banana peppers

Stuffed Banana Peppers With Avocado Dip

6 banana peppers, cut lengthwise into halves
2 c. white vinegar
1½ c. avocado dip, page 190
¼ c. fresh chive, chopped

Under running cold water, rinse and remove seeds from cut peppers, using rubber gloves. Arrange peppers in a square dish. Pour vinegar over peppers; cover and refrigerate 6 hours or overnight. Turn peppers occasionally to absorb vinegar. Drain peppers and pat dry with paper towels. Fill peppers with avocado dip. Arrange on a flat platter and garnish with chopped chives.

Baked Egg Rolls

9 sheets phyllo pastry, thawed if frozen
Vegetable cooking spray
Vegetable filling, page 189

Place1 sheet phyllo pastry on a clean dry surface. Spray sheet with cooking spray. Place second sheet and spray; top with third sheet and spray. Cut into three squares. Place a little filling in the middle on each square. Spray around edges. Fold sides first, roll to form a roll. Spray baking sheet; place rolls seam side down, cover with damp towel and set aside. Repeat with rest of phyllo. Preheat oven to 400 degrees (F), spray rolls and prick tops with fork for steam to escape. Bake 25 minutes or until golden brown. Serve with coriander chutney, page 201.

Note:
When cooking with phyllo, always work quickly. Also place a
damp towel on the rest of the phyllo so that it won't dry out.

Vegetable Phyllo Bags

2 T. olive oil
1 sm. onion, chopped
1 c. green onions, chopped
1 c. shredded carrots
1 med. potato, boiled, peeled and mashed
Lemon pepper to taste
¼ c. fresh parsley, chopped
9 sheet phyllo pastry, thawed if frozen
Vegetable cooking spray

Heat nonstick skillet on medium high heat, add oil; sauté onions, green onions and carrots. Add mashed potato, sauté 2 to 3 minutes and add lemon pepper to taste. Add parsley and mix well. Remove from heat and set aside to cool. Place 1 sheet of phyllo on dry surface; spray sheet with vegetable spray. Place second sheet and spray, top with a third sheet and spray. Cut into 4 squares or any size you prefer. Place a teaspoon of vegetable mixture in center of each square; gather up edges to form a small bag. Twist the top and press to seal. Repeat with remaining sheets and filling. Spray phyllo bags; place on prepared baking sheet. Bake in preheated oven at 400 degrees (F) for 25 minutes or until golden brown. Transfer to a platter; serve with chutney or sauce.

Note:
Cover filled phyllo bags with damp towel and repeat
with rest of phyllo dough and filling.

Baked Jackfruit Rolls

1 (20-oz.) can young green Jackfruit, drained and rinsed
2 med. potatoes
1 sm. onion, chopped
2 cloves garlic, minced
1 thinly sliced fresh ginger, crushed and minced
1 T. vegetables curry powder, page 196
2 T. fresh parsley, minced
Lemon pepper to taste
9 sheets phyllo pastry, thawed if frozen
Vegetable cooking spray

Combine Jackfruit and potatoes in a pan. Cover with water 1-inch above vegetables. On high heat, bring to boil; reduce to medium heat. Cover and cook until tender. Drain water. Mash jackfruit and potatoes with the back of a wooden spoon. Add onion, garlic, ginger, vegetable curry powder and parsley; mix well. Add lemon pepper to taste. Mash with spoon to combine flavors; set aside. Place 1 sheet phyllo on dry surface; spray sheet with vegetable spray. Place second sheet and spray; top with third sheet and spray. Cut into 3 squares. Place a little filling in middle of each square. Spray around edges. Fold sides inside first, and roll to form a roll. Spray baking sheet with vegetable spray; place rolls seam side down. Cover with a damp towel; set aside. Repeat until phyllo and filling is used up. Preheat oven to 400(F), spray rolls; prick tops with fork for steam to escape. Bake for 25 minutes or until golden brown.

Note:
When cooking with phyllo, always work
quickly and place a damp towel over rest of the
dough so it won't dry out.

Jackfruit Cutlets

1 (20-oz.) can young green Jackfruit, drained and rinsed, or fresh young Jackfruit
2 med. potatoes, peeled and cubed
1 T. vegetable oil
1 sm. onion, chopped
2 cloves garlic, minced
1 thin sliced fresh ginger, minced
2 egg yolks
Salt, pepper and limejuice to taste
6 egg whites, beaten
10 oz. seasoned breadcrumbs
Vegetable oil for frying

Into a pan, add Jackfruit and potatoes, cover with water to 1-inch above. On high heat, bring to a boil. Reduce to medium heat, cover and cook until tender. Drain water and set aside. Heat a skillet on medium-high heat; sauté onion, garlic, ginger and parsley, add combine Jackfruit and potato. Remove from heat and set aside cool. Transfer to food processor, add egg yolks, process 1 minute. Add salt, pepper and limejuice to taste. Process until it becomes a smooth mixture. Transfer to a bowl. Make small balls or any size you prefer. Using hands, dip each ball in beaten egg whites one at a time. Coat each ball with breadcrumbs and set aside. Heat a shallow pan or deep fryer, pour in enough oil. On medium-heat, let oil bubble. Add cutlets in batches and deep fry until golden brown; transfer onto paper towel. Serve cutlets with chutney or sauce.

Note:
Always use fresh oil to fry cutlets.

Please see photo at back of book.

Grandma's Pattie Dough

(And How To Make Patties)

2 c. all purpose flour
¾ tsp. salt
2 T. butter
1 egg yolk (reserve white for brushing)
¾ c. thick coconut milk
Vegetable oil for frying
Reserve additional flour and milk if necessary
Vegetables filling, page 189

On floured surface, sift flour and salt together. Make a well. Add butter and egg yolk. Mix with hands, gradually add milk and knead well. Add more flour or milk if necessary. Continue to knead until dough holds together to form a soft ball, which feels elastic and easy to work and does not stick. If sticky, add more flour and knead slightly. Wrap dough in foil or waxed paper; set aside to rest for at least ½ hour. Cut dough into portions, dust more flour on surface. Roll out 1 portion with rolling pin to form a sheet, sprinkle with flour, turn sheet over and do the same. Cut 3-inch circles or any size you prefer. Place a teaspoon of vegetable filling on each one. Brush around filling with reserved egg white. Fold in half and press. Seal with fork. Sprinkle flour on baking sheet and arrange patties. Continue to do the same until all dough and filling is used up. Deep fry patties in batches, until golden brown. Transfer patties onto paper towels. Serve with chutney or sauce.

Note:
Always use fresh oil to fry patties.

Sri Lankan Vegetable Roll Batter

(And How To Make Egg Rolls)

1½ c. all-purpose flour
½ tsp. salt (add more if desired)
1 egg yolk (reserve egg white for brushing)
2 c. cold water (add more if needed)
Vegetable filling, page 189
¼ c. canola oil for greasing pan
4 eggs, beaten slightly for coating egg rolls
10 oz. seasoned breadcrumbs

In a bowl, combine flour, salt and egg yolk. Gradually add water and whisk or blend to a smooth batter, to the consistency of a thin cream to coat spoon. Cover and chill until vegetable filling is prepared. Let batter stand 5 minutes at room temperature before using. If batter is too thick, add more water to thin. Place a 6-inch nonstick skillet on medium-high heat. Using a paper towel or cheesecloth, dip in oil slightly, and coat skillet. Lift skillet immediately; pour in a little batter (about ¼ cup) and swirl skillet around in a circular motion, until batter spreads evenly to form a crepe. Immediately return skillet to medium heat; cook until top of the crepe is set and underside of crepe is slightly golden brown. Do not turn crepe over. Using a spatula, gently loosen sides and transfer crepe to a flat platter. Immediately repeat by rubbing oil to skillet, return to heat, pour batter and cook crepes. While the next crepe is cooking, immediately place a little filling in middle of already cooked crepe. Brush edges around with egg white, fold in side first and roll carefully, set aside. Repeat process of making rolls until all the batter and filling is over. Dip rolls in egg whites and coat with breadcrumbs one at a time. Heat wok or deep fryer; pour enough oil to make sure oil will cover rolls. On high heat, let oil bubble. Deep fry rolls in batches, do not overcrowd. When rolls are golden brown, transfer to paper towels.

Note:
Rolls can be made and frozen. First place pre-fried rolls on baking tray. Freeze. When rolls are frozen, transfer to freezer bags. Seal well and freeze. Before using, thaw and deep fry.

Please see photo at back of book.

Coconut Milk Pattie Dough

2 c. all-purpose flour
¾ tsp. salt
1 egg yolk (reserve egg white for brushing)
¾ c. coconut milk
Vegetable oil for frying
Reserve additional flour and milk on side if necessary
Vegetable filling, page 189

On clean surface, sift flour and salt together. Make a well and add the egg yolk. Gradually add the milk and knead with hand, adding more flour and milk, if necessary, until dough holds together to form a soft ball, which feels elastic and easy to work with, and not sticky. Add more flour if dough is sticky. Knead dough slightly. Wrap dough with waxed paper or foil; set aside to rest for 20 minutes.

Cut dough into small portions on floured surface. Roll out 1 portion with rolling pin to form a sheet. Sprinkle with flour, turn dough over and do the same. Cut rounds into 3-inch circles, or ay size you prefer. Place a little filling in middle of circle. Brush around with egg wash; fold in half and press, sealing with fork.

Sprinkle flour on baking sheet. Arrange patties. Continue to do the same until dough is used. Deep fry patties in batches until golden brown. Transfer patties onto paper towel. Serve with chutney.

Beverages

Passion Fruit Cooler

6 ripe passion fruits
10 c. water
Pinch salt
Sugar to taste, if desired

Cut passion fruits in half. Using a teaspoon, scoop the pulp with seeds into blender. Add water and blend. Strain into a pitcher and discard pulp and seeds. Add salt and stir. Chill before serving. Add sugar, if desired.

Barley Water

½ c. quick Quaker barley, rinsed
10 c. water

In a saucepan, combine barley and water. On high heat, bring to a boil; reduce to medium heat. Cover and cook until barley is tender, stirring occasionally. Remove from heat; set aside to cool. Strain barley water into a pitcher and chill in refrigerator. Do not discard cooked barley seeds; freeze the barley seeds in freezer bags and use it for breakfast with a touch of brown sugar, or use in soups or salads.

Note:
great thirst quencher on a hot summer day!

Barley Orange Juice

½ c. quick Quaker barley, rinsed
8 c. water
4 c. freshly squeezed orange juice

Combine barley and water in saucepan. On high heat, bring to a boil. Reduce to medium heat, cover and cook until barley is tender, stirring occasionally. Remove from heat, cool barley. Strain barley water to a pitcher. Chill in refrigerator. Do not discard barley seeds. Freeze in freezer bags for soup. Add orange juice to barley water before serving.

Ginger Tea

1 T. loose tea or 2 regular tea bags
1 thin sliced fresh peeled ginger, washed and crushed
1½ c. boiling water
Sugar or honey

Warm the teapot by rinsing with boiling water. Place the loose tea in a tea ball. Place the tea ball or tea bags inside the teapot. Add the crushed ginger. Immediately pour boiling water. Stir, cover teapot and let steep for 7 minutes. Uncover, stir with sugar or honey.

Note:
Proper brewing is essential for flavor.

Ice Fruit Tea

10 c. fresh cold water
6 regular size black tea bags
4 regular size raspberry tea bags
4 regular size peach tea bags
Sliced lemon for garnish

Pour fresh cold water into a large saucepan. Cover and bring to a boil on high heat. Turn off heat and uncover. Immediately add the tea bags, cover and let steep for 20 minutes. Uncover and discard tea bags. Cool tea completely. Pour into a large pitcher and chill in refrigerator. Pour into a tall glass with ice cubes; garnish with sliced lemon.

Note:
Proper brewing is essential for flavor.

Tropical Fruit Ice Tea

12 c. fresh cold water
6 regular size mango tea bags
4 regular size pineapple tea bags
4 regular size passion fruit tea bags
4 regular size black tea bags
Sliced lemon for garnish

Pour fresh cold water into a large saucepan, cover and bring to boil on high heat. Turn off heat and uncover. Immediately add the tea bags, cover and let steep 20 minutes. Uncover and discard tea bags. Cool tea completely. Pour into a large pitcher. Chill in refrigerator. Pour into a tall glass with ice cubes and garnish with sliced lemon.

Note:
Proper brewing is essential for flavor.

Beverages

Morning Glory

2 apples, peeled, cored and diced
2 carrots, peeled and diced
1 stalk celery
2 c. diced cucumber
1 c. fresh parsley, trimmed and washed well
½ tsp. lemon juice

    Process all ingredients in juicer or blender to a smooth consistency. Strain through a wire sieve; serve immediately.

Red Booster

1 c. fresh cherries, pitted and rinsed
1 c. fresh raspberries, rinsed
1 c. fresh strawberries, rinsed
1 c. fresh blood orange juice
Crushed ice

    Blend all the ingredients to a smooth consistency; serve immediately.

Cherimoya Smoothie

1 ripe cherimoya
1 tsp. lemon juice
½ c. vanilla yogurt
Crushed ice

    Cut cherimoya in half; remove seeds. Using a teaspoon, scoop out flesh and transfer into a blender. Add the lemon juice, yogurt and crushed ice. Blend to a smooth consistency; serve immediately.

19

Avocado Smoothie

1 large ripe avocado, halved and stoned
1 tsp. lemon juice
½ c. vanilla yogurt
Crushed ice

Using a small teaspoon, scoop out flesh; transfer into blender. Add lemon juice, yogurt and crushed ice. Blend to a smooth consistency; serve immediately.

Ice Coffee

16 c. water (1 gallon)
1 c. Nescafe instant coffee
2 cans (14 oz) condensed milk
2 T. pure vanilla extract
1 c. sugar
¼ c. brandy (opt.)

In a pan bring water to a boil. Remove from heat, add instant coffee and stir until dissolved. Next, add the rest of the ingredients, stir well until condensed milk and sugar are completely dissolved. Pour into a pitcher and set a side to cool, chill in refrigerator until ready to serve.

Note.
It's great for a party or a summer drink.

Vegetables

Spicy Eggplant In Mustard Sauce

2 med. eggplant
1¼ c. water
1 T. cayenne
¼ c. onions, chopped
2 cloves garlic, crushed
Garlic salt to taste
2 c. coconut milk or soymilk
2 T. country Dijon mustard

Wash eggplant. Slice and cut into pieces crossways. In a nonstick saucepan, combine eggplant and rest of the ingredients except milk and mustard; stir. On high heat, bring to boil; reduce to medium heat. Cover and cook until eggplant is tender and water is absorbed, stirring occasionally. Add milk and mustard; stir. Reduce to low heat. Uncover and simmer until thick. Remove from heat. Serve with rice.

Lentils With Watercress

1 c. red lentils
¼ c. onions, chopped
2 c. water
Dash of turmeric powder
Garlic salt to taste
2 bunches of watercress
2 c. coconut milk or soymilk

Discard tough stems, discolored or spoiled leaves. Wash well to remove sand. Drain water and set aside. In a nonstick saucepan, combine lentils, onions, water and turmeric. Add garlic salt to taste. On high heat bring to a boil. Reduce to low heat, cover and cook until lentils are tender and water is absorbed, stirring occasionally. Add watercress and milk and stir. Uncover and simmer until thick. Remove from heat and serve with rice.

Artichoke Potato Curry

1 (14-oz.) can artichoke drained
¼ c. onion, chopped
1 med. tomato chopped
1 med. potato, boiled and cubed
2 cloves garlic, chopped
1 T. paprika
1 T. roasted curry powder, page 198
2 c. coconut milk or soymilk
Salt to taste

In nonstick saucepan, combine artichoke and rest of the ingredients. Add salt to taste. On high heat, bring to boil. Reduce to low heat, uncover and simmer until thick, stirring occasionally. Remove from heat and serve with rice.

Potato And Eggplant Curry

2 med. potatoes, with skin, cut into cubes
1 med. eggplant, washed and cut into cubes
1 med. tomato, chopped
¼ c. onion, chopped
2 cloves garlic, chopped
Dash turmeric powder
2 T. tomato paste
2 T. mild curry paste, page 196
2 c. water
1 ½ c. coconut milk or soymilk
1 T. fresh parsley, chopped
Salt to taste

In a nonstick saucepan, combine potatoes and rest of the ingredients, except milk, parsley and salt. On high heat, bring to boil; reduce to medium heat. Cover and cook until tender, stirring occasionally. Add milk, parsley and salt. Reduce to low heat. Uncover and simmer until thick, stirring occasionally. Remove from heat and serve with rice.

Leek Curry

1 Bunch leeks
1 sm. onion, chopped
2 cloves garlic, crushed
1 T. paprika
2 T. tomato paste
1 T. country Dijon mustard
1 ½ c. coconut milk or soymilk
Salt to taste

Discard roots and discolored spoiled leaves. Wash well to remove sand and drain water. Finley slice leeks. In a nonstick saucepan, combine leeks and rest of the ingredients. On high heat, bring to a boil. Reduce to medium heat. Uncover and simmer until thick, stirring occasionally. Remove from heat and serve with rice.

Pumpkin Curry With Curry Paste

2 lbs. pumpkin, seeded and cut into sm. chunks with skin
¼ c. onion, chopped
2 cloves garlic, chopped
1 med. tomato, chopped
2 T. mild curry paste, page 196
1 ¾ c. water or stock
Garlic salt to taste
2 c. coconut milk or soymilk
1 T. fresh parsley, chopped

In nonstick saucepan, combine pumpkin and rest of the ingredients except milk and parsley. On high heat; bring to boil; reduce to medium heat. Cover and cook until tender. Add milk and parsley; stir. Reduce to low heat. Uncover and simmer until thick, stirring occasionally. Remove from heat; serve with rice and parsley salad.

Lentils With Spinach

1 c. red lentils
2 c. water
¼ c. onion, chopped
2 cloves garlic, chopped
Dash turmeric powder
Garlic salt to taste
1 (10-oz.) pkg. Frozen chopped spinach, thawed and drained
1 c. coconut milk or soymilk

Wash lentils well 3 or 4 times; drain water. In a nonstick saucepan, combine lentils, water, onions, garlic, turmeric and garlic salt. Stir. On high heat, bring to a boil. Reduce to low heat. Cover and cook until tender and all the water is absorbed, stirring occasionally. Add spinach and milk; stir. Uncover and simmer until thick, stirring occasionally. Remove from heat and serve with rice.

Stir-fry Tomatoes

12 cherry tomatoes, halved
1 med. onion, halved and finely sliced
2 T. Cajun seasoning
2 T. tomato paste
¼ c. fresh basil, chopped
Salt to taste
2 T. vegetable oil

In a bowl combine tomatoes and rest of the ingredients except vegetable oil. Mix and set aside. Heat a nonstick skillet until warm. Add oil and heat. On medium heat, add mixed ingredients. Stir-fry for 5 minutes. Reduce to low heat. Cover and simmer until liquid is absorbed, stirring occasionally. Remove from heat. Serve inside pita bread, on sliced bagels or on soft tacos.

Stir-fry Tofu

2 T. vegetable oil
1 med. onion, halved and finely sliced
2 green chili peppers, seeded and sliced
½ c. fresh mushrooms sliced
1 c. cherry tomatoes, halved
1 tsp. Cajun seasoning
1 tsp. dried cilantro or 1 T. fresh cilantro
1 (16-oz.) pkg. Tofu, drained and cut into cubes
Dash hot pepper sauce

Heat oil in a nonstick skillet. On medium heat, sauté onions, chili peppers, mushrooms and tomatoes. Add Cajun seasoning and cilantro. Sauté for a few minutes, add tofu and hot pepper sauce. Stir-fry for 3 minutes. Remove from heat and serve immediately with rice.

Zucchini Curry

3 med. zucchini, washed, cut in 1 ½ -in. pieces lengthwise
¼ c. onions, chopped
2 cloves garlic, crushed
¼ c. tomato paste
½ tsp. dried basil
½ tsp. dried thyme
Dash turmeric powder
2 T. country Dijon mustard
2 c. coconut milk or soymilk
Salt to taste

In a nonstick skillet, combine zucchini and the rest of the ingredients. On high heat, bring to a boil. Reduce to medium heat; uncover and cook until tender, stirring occasionally. Remove from heat and serve with rice.

Yellow Split Pea Curry

1 c. yellow split peas
2 c. water
Dash turmeric powder
Garlic salt to taste
1 T. vegetable oil
¼ c. onions, chopped
2 cloves garlic, chopped
1 T. roasted curry powder, page 198
1 ¾ c. coconut milk or soymilk

Wash split peas well 3 or 4 times and drain water. In a nonstick saucepan, combine split peas, water and turmeric. Add garlic salt to taste. On high heat, bring to a boil. Reduce to low heat. Cover and cook until tender and all the water is absorbed, stirring occasionally. Remove from heat and transfer to a bowl. Return saucepan to medium heat, add oil and heat. Add onions, garlic and roasted curry powder, sauté for 2 minutes. Add cooked split peas, sauté for 2 minutes. Add milk and stir. Reduce to low heat, uncover and simmer until thick, stirring occasionally. Remove from heat serve with rice and a salad.

Yellow Potato Curry

3 med. potatoes, peeled and cut into cubes
¼ tsp. turmeric powder
¼ c. onions, chopped
2 cloves garlic, chopped
1 med. tomato, chopped
Bay leaf
2 c. water
2 c. coconut milk or soymilk
¼ c. fresh parsley, chopped
Garlic salt to taste

In a nonstick saucepan, combine potatoes and rest of the ingredients except milk, parsley and garlic salt. On high heat, bring to a boil. Reduce to medium heat. Cover and cook until potatoes are tender, stirring occasionally. Remove bay leaf and discard. Add milk parsley and garlic salt to taste. Uncover and simmer until gravy is thick, stirring occasionally. Serve with rice and parsley salad.

Four Vegetables In One Pot

1 lg. Sweet potato, peeled and cut into med. chunks
½ c. red lentils, washed 3 or 4 times, and drained*
¼ c. onions, chopped
Dash turmeric powder
1 tsp. paprika
2 c. water
Garlic salt to taste
2 med. carrots, sliced
3 c. fresh spinach, washed
1 ¾ c. coconut milk or soymilk

In a nonstick saucepan, combine the first 7 ingredients. On high heat, bring to a boil. Reduce to medium heat. Cover and cook sweet potato and red lentils until tender. Add carrots. Cover and cook until tender. Add spinach and milk. Reduce to low heat. Uncover and simmer until thick, stirring occasionally. Remove from heat and serve with rice.

Giant Beans In Tomato Sauce

2 c. giant beans
2 T. olive oil
1 med. red onion, halved and finely sliced
¼ c. tomato paste
1 (14-oz.) can tomatoes, diced with juice
1 T. mild curry paste, page 196
1 tsp. dried parsley
1 tsp. dried thyme
1 tsp. dried oregano
¼ c. fresh basil, chopped
Garlic salt to taste

Wash beans. Add beans into a nonstick saucepan. Cover with water, 3 to 4 inches above beans. Let soak overnight. Discard any skins and beans that float on top. Drain water. Pour fresh water over beans again, 3 to 4 inches above. On high heat, bring to a boil. Reduce to medium heat. Cover and cook until beans are tender. Drain water. Transfer beans to a bowl. Return saucepan to medium heat. Add oil, heat and sauté onions until transparent. Add the rest of the ingredients. Stir. Add beans. Reduce to low heat. Cover and simmer until thick. Remove from heat. Serve with rice or pasta.

Endive Stir-fry

1 lb. endive
1 T. chili powder
Garlic salt to taste
2 T. vegetable oil
¼ c. onions, chopped
1 med. tomato, chopped
2 T. tomato paste

Discard spoiled or discolored leaves. Wash well to remove any sand, drain water. Pat dry leaves with paper towels. Finely shred endive. In a bowl, combine endive and chili powder. Mix. Add garlic salt to taste and set aside. Heat a nonstick skillet until warm. Add oil and heat. On medium heat, sauté onions, tomatoes and tomato paste for 2 minutes. Add mixed endive and stir-fry until liquid is absorbed. Remove from heat and serve with rice and a curried dish.

Eggplant In Mustard Sauce

1 med. eggplant
1¼ c. water
Dash turmeric powder
¼ c. onions, chopped
2 cloves garlic, crushed
1 bay leaf
Salt to taste
2 c. coconut milk or soymilk
2 T. country Dijon mustard

Wash eggplant, slice diagonally into pieces. In a nonstick saucepan, combine eggplant and the rest of the ingredients except milk and mustard. Stir. On high heat, bring to boil. Reduce to medium heat. Cover and cook until water is absorbed, stirring occasionally. Add milk and mustard and stir. Reduce to low heat. Uncover and simmer until thick. Remove from heat and serve with rice.

String Bean Curry

1 lb. fresh beans, ends broken off and string removed; may substitute frozen beans
¼ c. onions, chopped
2 cloves garlic, chopped
1 med. tomato, chopped
Dash turmeric powder
Dash paprika
½ c. water
Garlic salt to taste
1 ¾ c. coconut milk or soymilk

Break beans into 1-inch pieces. In a nonstick saucepan, combine beans and the rest of the ingredients except milk. On high heat, bring to a boil. Reduce to medium heat. Cover and cook until tender and all the water is absorbed. Add milk and stir. Reduce to low heat. Uncover and simmer until thick, stirring occasionally. Serve with a curried dish.

String Bean Stir-fry

1 lb. tender string beans, strings removed and broken into 1-in. pieces
Dash turmeric powder
1 tsp. Cajun seasoning
½ c. water
1 ½ T. vegetable oil
¼ c. onions, chopped
1 sm. tomato, chopped

In a nonstick skillet, combine the first 4 ingredients. On high heat, bring to a boil. Reduce to medium heat. Cover and cook until water is absorbed. Remove from heat. Transfer to a bowl and set aside. Return skillet to medium heat. Add oil and heat, sauté onions and tomatoes for 2 minutes. Add cooked beans and stir-fry until liquid is absorbed. Remove from heat and serve with rice.

Portobello Mushrooms With Lentils

3 med. Portobello mushrooms
1 c. cooked lentils
¼ c. onion, chopped
2 cloves garlic, chopped
1 med. tomato, chopped
1 ½ T. paprika
1 tsp. roasted curry powder, page 198
2 ½ c. coconut milk or soymilk
Lemon pepper to taste

Using a wet paper towel, clean caps of mushrooms. Hold the mushrooms upright and carefully scrape off gills with a small spoon. Cut into thick slices; set aside. In a nonstick shallow skillet, combine mushrooms and rest of the ingredients; stir. On high heat, bring to a boil; reduce to low heat. Cover and simmer until mushrooms are tender, stirring occasionally. Serve over rice or pasta.

Cucumber In Yellow Mustard Sauce

4 med. cucumbers
¼ c. onion, chopped
Dash fresh peeled grated ginger
2 cloves garlic, chopped
1 T. vegetable curry powder, page 196 or dash turmeric powder
1 ½ c. water
1 ½ c. coconut milk or soymilk
2 T. country Dijon mustard

Peel cucumbers; cut in half lengthwise. Using a small spoon, scoop out seeds. Cut diagonal slices. Combine first 6 ingredients in a nonstick shallow skillet. On high heat, bring to a boil; reduce to medium heat. Cover and cook until cucumber is slightly tender and water is absorbed, stirring occasionally. Add milk and mustard; stir. Uncover and simmer until sauce is slightly thick, stirring occasionally.

Curried Daikon (White Radish)

1½ lbs. tender Daikon, peeled and thickly sliced
¼ c. onion, chopped
2 cloves garlic, chopped
Dash fresh peeled grated ginger
1 sm. green chili, seeded and sliced
1 T. paprika
1 T. roasted curry powder, page 198
1 med. tomato, chopped
2½ c. coconut milk or soymilk
Lemon pepper to taste

In nonstick shallow skillet, combine Daikon and rest of the ingredients. On high heat, bring to a boil; cover and cook 5 minutes. Uncover, stir and simmer until Daikon is tender and curry is slightly thick. Remove from heat and serve with rice.

Pumpkin Curry

2 lbs. pumpkin, seeded and cut into chunks with skin
¼ c. onion, chopped
2 cloves garlic, chopped
1 thin slice fresh ginger, peeled, crushed and minced
1 sm. green chili, seeded and minced
Dash curry leaves
1½ T. paprika
1½ T roasted curry powder, page 198
Dash of cayenne pepper
2 c. water
Lemon pepper to taste
1½ c. coconut milk or soymilk

In nonstick shallow skillet, combine pumpkin and rest of the ingredients except milk. On high heat, bring to a boil; reduce to medium heat. Cover and cook until tender, stirring occasionally. Add milk; uncover and simmer until sauce is slightly thick. Serve over rice.

Carrot Curry

3 med. carrots, peeled and sliced
¼ c. onion, chopped
2 cloves garlic, chopped
Dash fresh peeled grated ginger
1 sm. green chili, seeded and chopped
1 T. paprika
1 T. roasted curry powder, page 198
1¾ c. coconut milk or soymilk
Lemon pepper to taste

In nonstick shallow skillet, combine carrots and rest of the ingredients. On high heat, bring to a boil; reduce to medium heat. Cover and cook for 5 minutes. Uncover and simmer until curry is slightly thick, stirring occasionally. Remove from heat; serve with rice.

Roasted Red Bell Pepper Curry

6 med. firm red bell peppers
¼ c. onion, chopped
2 cloves garlic, chopped
¼ tsp. fresh ginger, minced
¼ tsp. fresh green chili, seeded and minced
2 T. mild curry paste, page 196
2½ c. coconut milk or soymilk
Salt to taste
¼ c. fresh parsley, chopped

Char bell peppers over gas flame, holding with tongs, turning bell peppers until blistered and charred on all sides or char under broiler. Transfer peppers immediately into a paper bag and close to seal. Let stand 10 minutes. To peel peppers, use a wet paper towel to rub off skin. Cut in half; discard cores, ribs and seeds. Place peppers in a nonstick shallow skillet. Add rest of the ingredients. On high heat, bring to a boil; reduce to medium heat. Uncover and simmer until curry is thick.

Lentils With Artichoke In Yellow Curry Sauce

1 c. red lentils
2 c. water
¼ c. onion, chopped
2 cloves garlic, chopped
1 thin slice fresh ginger, peeled and minced
I med. tomato, chopped
2 T. vegetable curry powder, page 196
1 (14-oz.) can artichoke hearts, drained and rinsed
2 c. coconut milk or soymilk
lemon pepper to taste

Wash lentils 3 or 4 times; drain water. In nonstick shallow skillet, combine lentils, water, onion, garlic, tomato and vegetable curry powder. On high heat, bring to a boil; reduce to medium heat. Cover and cook until slightly tender, stirring occasionally. Discard any foam that floats on top. Add artichokes and milk. Stir. Add lemon pepper to taste. Uncover and simmer until slightly thick.

Oven Roasted Tomato Curry

6 med. firm red tomatoes, halved
2 T. olive oil or canola oil
Dash lemon pepper
¼ c. chopped onion
2 cloves garlic, chopped
1 green chili pepper, chopped
2 T. paprika
2 T. roasted curry powder, page 198
2 c. coconut milk or soymilk
Salt to taste
¼ c. fresh basil leaf, shredded

Preheat oven to 400(F) degrees. Brush base of pan with oil. Place tomatoes cut side up, season with lemon pepper. Drizzle with remaining oil over tomatoes. Roast for 30 minutes until slightly soft and edges are slightly charred but not burned. Remove from heat, transfer tomatoes with juices in to a shallow skillet. Add rest of the ingredients except basil. On high heat bring to a boil. Reduce to low heat, cover and simmer until curry is slightly thick, carefully turning tomatoes occasionally. Remove from heat. Add basil, cover and let stand for 5 minutes. Serve with rice or pasta.

Chickpea Curry

2 c. cooked chickpeas, page 89
¼ c. onion, chopped
2 cloves garlic, chopped
Dash fresh peeled grated ginger
1 sm. green chili, seeded and chopped
1 med. tomato, chopped
¼ c. tomato sauce
2 T. paprika
2 T. roasted curry powder, page 198
2½ c. coconut milk or soymilk
Lemon pepper to taste

In nonstick shallow skillet, combine chickpeas and rest of the ingredients. On high heat, bring to a boil; reduce to medium heat. Uncover and simmer until curry is slightly thick, stirring occasionally.

Carrots In Yellow Curry Sauce

4 med. carrots, peeled and sliced diagonally
¼ c. onion, chopped
2 cloves garlic, chopped
Dash fresh peeled grated ginger
1 sm. green chili, seeded and chopped
2½ c. coconut milk or soymilk
Dash turmeric powder
Pinch of fenugreek seeds
Lemon pepper to taste
¼ c. fresh parsley

In nonstick shallow skillet, combine carrots and rest of the ingredients except parsley. On high heat, bring to a boil; reduce to medium heat. Cover and cook for 5 minutes. Uncover and simmer until carrots are tender, stirring occasionally. Add parsley; simmer until curry is slightly thick. Remove from heat; serve with rice.

Curried Beets And Greens

1 bunch of tender beets with greens
2 T. paprika
1 T. vegetable curry powder, page 196
¼ c. onion, chopped
2 cloves garlic, chopped
Dash fresh peeled grated ginger
1½ c. water
Lemon pepper to taste
1½ c. coconut milk or soymilk

Separate greens from beets; discard discolored and spoiled leaves and tough stems. Rinse a few times under running cold water to remove sand; transfer to colander to drain water. Rinse and scrub beets under running cold water. Peel and dice beets. Chop greens and stems into large pieces; set aside. In nonstick shallow skillet, combine diced beets and rest of the ingredients except milk, chopped green and stems. On high heat, bring to a boil. Reduce to medium heat. Cover and cook until water is absorbed, stirring occasionally. Uncover, add milk, chopped greens and stems; stir. Add more lemon pepper to taste if needed. Simmer until curry is slightly thick, stirring occasionally. Remove from heat and serve with rice.

Curried Soy Beans

3 c. cooked soy beans, page 97
2½ c. coconut milk or soymilk
¼ c. onion, chopped
2 cloves garlic, chopped
Dash fresh peeled grated ginger
1 med. tomato, chopped
1 sm. green chili, seeded and chopped
2 T. paprika
1½ T. roasted curry powder, page 198
Lemon pepper to taste

Combine all ingredients in a nonstick shallow skillet. On high heat, bring to a boil. Reduce to medium heat. Uncover and simmer until curry is slightly thick, stirring occasionally. Remove from heat serve with rice or pasta.

Spicy Curried Cashew Nut Curry

2 c. fresh raw cashew nuts
¼ c. onion, chopped
2 cloves garlic, chopped
Dash fresh peeled grated ginger
1 sm. green chili, seeded and chopped
1 T. paprika
½ c. tsp. cayenne pepper
1 T. roasted curry powder, page 198
2 c. coconut milk or soymilk
Lemon pepper to taste

Combine cashew nuts and rest of the ingredients in a nonstick shallow skillet. On high heat, bring to a boil. Reduce to medium heat. Uncover and simmer until cashew nuts are tender, stirring occasionally. Remove from heat and serve with rice

Sauteed Carrots

3 med. carrots, peeled and julienned
1 T. paprika
Lime juice and salt to taste
3 T. olive oil or vegetable oil
1 sm. red onion, chopped
1 sm. green chili, seeded and chopped
¼ c. fresh parsley, chopped
More lime juice and salt to taste

In a bowl, combine carrots and paprika; add lime juice and salt to taste. Set aside. Place a nonstick shallow skillet on medium heat. Add oil and heat, sauté onions and chili. Add combined carrots; cover and cook for 5 minutes. Uncover and add parsley. Sauté until liquid is absorbed, stirring constantly. Add more limejuice and salt to taste, if needed. Remove from heat and serve with rice.

Curried Jicama

2 med. tender jicama, peeled, and diced
¼ c. onion, chopped
2 cloves garlic, chopped
Dash fresh peeled grated ginger
1 sm. green chili, seeded and chopped
1 T. paprika
1 T. roasted curry powder, page 198
1 med. tomato, chopped
2 c. coconut milk or soymilk
Lemon pepper to taste

In nonstick shallow saucepan, combine jicama and rest of the ingredients. On high heat, bring to a boil. Reduce to medium heat. Cover and cook for 10 minutes. Uncover and simmer until jicama is tender and curry is slightly thick, stirring occasionally. Remove from heat and serve with rice.

Daikon In A Yellow Mustard Curry Sauce

2½ c. tender Daikon, peeled, and diced
¼ c. onion, chopped
2 cloves garlic, chopped
Dash fresh peeled grated ginger
1 T. vegetable curry powder, page 196 or dash turmeric powder
2½ c. coconut milk or soymilk
Lemon pepper to taste
2 T. country Dijon mustard

In nonstick shallow skillet, combine Daikon and rest of the ingredients except mustard. On high heat, bring to a boil. Reduce to medium heat. Cover and cook for 5 minutes. Uncover; stir. Add mustard, simmer until Daikon is tender and curry is slightly thick, stirring occasionally. Serve with rice.

Cabbage In Curried Mustard Sauce

½ head of cabbage, use white and green leaves
¼ c. onion, chopped
2 cloves garlic, chopped
Dash fresh peeled grated ginger
1 sm. green chili, seeded and chopped
1 T. vegetable curry powder, page 196 or dash turmeric powder
2 c. coconut milk or soymilk
Lemon pepper to taste
2 T. county Dijon mustard

Wash cabbage; cut into quarters. First slice off core then slice cabbage and set aside. In a nonstick shallow skillet, combine sliced cabbage and rest of the ingredients except mustard. On high heat, bring to a boil. Reduce to medium heat. Cover and cook for 5 minutes. Uncover and add mustard. Stir. Simmer until cabbage is tender and curry is thick, stirring occasionally. Remove from heat; serve with rice.

Sauteed Turnips With Greens

1 bunch tender turnips with greens
1 T. paprika
¾ c. water
Lemon pepper to taste
2 T. olive oil or vegetable oil
1 sm. onion, chopped
Dash dry chili pepper flakes

Separate greens from turnips; discard discolored and spoiled leaves and tough stems. Rinse a few times under cold water to remove sand; place over colander to drain. Peel and wash turnips. Shred turnips and greens; chop stems. Transfer to a shallow nonstick skillet. Add paprika, water and lemon pepper to taste. Stir to combine. On high heat, bring to a boil. Reduce to medium heat. Cover and cook until water is absorbed, stirring occasionally. Remove from heat; transfer cooked turnip to a bowl, Return skillet to medium heat; add oil. Sauté onions for 2 minutes; add cooked turnips and chili pepper flakes. Sauté until liquid is absorbed, stirring constantly. Remove from heat; serve with rice.

Spiced Tofu Sauteed With Onions And Fresh Baby Spinach

3 T. olive oil or canola oil
1 med. onion halved and finely sliced
1 (16-oz.) pkg. firm tofu, drained and cut into slices
1 ½ T. paprika
Lemon pepper to taste
3 c. fresh baby spinach
Hot sauce to taste

Heat nonstick shallow skillet; add oil. On medium-high heat, sauté onions until slightly caramelized. Add tofu, paprika and lemon pepper to taste; stir. Cover and cook for 5 minutes. Uncover; add spinach and hot sauce to taste, stirring constantly, until spinach is wilted and liquid is absorbed. Remove from heat. Serve over rice or pasta.

Butternut Squash With Swiss Chard

2 lbs. butternut squash, peeled, seeded and cut into sm. chunks
¼ c. onion, chopped
2 cloves garlic, chopped
1 T. vegetable curry powder, page 196
2 c. water
Salt to taste
1½ c. coconut milk or soymilk
3 c. Swiss chard leaves and stems, cut into sm. pieces
2 T. country Dijon mustard

In nonstick shallow skillet, combine squash and rest of the ingredients except milk, Swiss chard and mustard. On high heat, bring to a boil; reduce to medium heat. Cover and cook until squash is slightly tender, stirring occasionally. Uncover; add milk, Swiss chard and mustard. Stir; simmer until Swiss chard is wilted. Add salt to taste. Remove from heat serve over rice or pasta.

Sauteed Daikon (White Radish)

1½ lbs. Daikon, peeled and julienned
1 T. paprika
Dash dry chili pepper
¼ c. water
1 tsp. lemon pepper
2 T. olive oil or vegetable oil
1 sm. onion, chopped
1 sm. green chili, seeded and chopped
More lemon pepper to taste
¼ c. fresh chives, chopped

In nonstick shallow skillet, combine Daikon, paprika, chili pepper flakes, water and lemon pepper. Stir to combine. On high heat, bring to a boil; reduce to medium heat; cover and cook until slightly tender and liquid is absorbed, stirring occasionally. Remove from heat; transfer cooked Daikon to a bowl; set aside. Return skillet to medium heat; add oil, heat and sauté onions and green chilies 2 minutes. Add cooked Daikon; add more lemon pepper to taste. Sauté until liquid is absorbed, stirring constantly. Add chives. Remove from heat; cover and let stand for flavors to blend. Serve with rice.

Healthy Deviled Tofu

1 (16-oz.) pkg. lite tofu, drained and cubed
1 T. paprika
1 T. hot sauce
Olive oil cooking spray
1 banana pepper or jalapeno, seeded and sliced
1 med. tomato, chopped
1 sm. onion, diced
Lemon pepper to taste

In a bowl, combine tofu, paprika and hot sauce. Heat nonstick shallow skillet; spray with cooking spray. Add peppers and tomatoes. Cover and cook until soft; uncover. Add onions and combine ingredients. Spray with cooking spray; sauté until liquid is absorbed, stirring occasionally without breaking tofu. Add lemon pepper to taste; stir. Cook until heated through; serve over rice.

Deviled Portobello Mushrooms With Carrots And Beets

2 med. firm Portobello mushrooms
3 T. olive oil or canola oil
1 banana pepper or jalapeno, seeded and sliced diagonally
1 med. tomato, diced
1 sm. red onion, diced
2 med. carrots, boiled, peeled and sliced diagonally
2 med. tender beets, boiled, peeled, halved and sliced
1 T. paprika
Lemon pepper to taste
¼ c. chopped parsley

Using wet paper towels, clean caps and hold mushrooms upright. Use a small spoon to scrape off gills. Slice mushrooms into thick slices; set aside. Place nonstick skillet on medium-high heat; add oil. Sauté peppers, tomato and onion for 2 minutes. Add mushrooms, cover and cook for 2 minutes. Uncover, add carrots, beets, paprika and lemon pepper. Sauté until liquid is absorbed, stirring constantly. Remove from heat; add parsley. Serve with rice.

Curried Lentil Tomato Sauce

1 ½ c. cooked red lentils
4 c. vegetable stock or water with 2 cubes vegetable bouillon
1 sm. onion, chopped
2 cloves garlic, minced
Dash fresh peeled grated ginger
2 T. paprika
2 T. roasted curry powder, page 198
1 tsp. Italian seasoning
2 med. tomatoes, halved, seeded and chopped
2 sm. green chili peppers, seeded and chopped
¼ c. tomato paste
1 c. tomato sauce
2 T. red vinegar
Lime juice and salt to taste
1/3 c. fresh parsley, chopped

In nonstick saucepan, combine lentils and rest of the ingredients except limejuice, salt and parsley. On high heat, bring to a boil. Reduce to medium-low heat, cover and simmer until sauce is slightly thick, stirring occasionally. Add limejuice and salt to taste. Add parsley and stir. Remove from heat. Cover and let stand for flavors to blend until ready to serve. Serve over rice or pasta.

Snake Gourd In Yellow Curry Sauce

2 lbs. snake gourd
¼ c. onion, chopped
2 cloves garlic, chopped
1 sm. green chili pepper, seeded and chopped
2 c. coconut milk or soymilk
Dash turmeric powder
Salt to taste
Dash roasted curry powder, page 198

Scrape off shiny skinny surface of snake gourd, slit in half, remove seeds and fibrous pulp. Rinse under cold running water. Cut slices diagonally. Transfer to nonstick shallow skillet. Add rest of the ingredients except roasted curry powder. On high heat, bring to boil; reduce to medium heat. Uncover and simmer until snake gourd is tender and curry is slightly thick, stirring occasionally. Remove from heat. Sprinkle with roasted curry powder, cover and let stand for flavors to blend until ready to serve. Serve with rice.

Stuffed Snake Gourd

1 med. size tender snake gourd (2 ½ to 3 ½ lbs.)
Potato cashew nut filling, page 195
3 T. olive oil or canola oil
1sm. green chili peppers, seeded and chopped
Dash fresh peeled grated ginger
2 T. paprika
1 T. vegetable curry powder, page 196
2½ c. coconut milk or soymilk
Lemon pepper to taste
1 tsp. roasted curry powder, page 198

Scrape off shiny skinny surface of snake gourd. Rinse under cold running water. Cut 1½ -inch pieces gently remove seeds and pulp; discard. Stuff pieces with filling; set aside. Place a nonstick shallow skillet in medium heat, uncover. Add oil; heat. Sauté stuffed pieces very carefully, turning few times. Transfer onto paper towels. Rinse skillet; add sautéed stuffed snake gourd and rest of the ingredients except roasted curry powder. On high heat bring to a boil. Reduce to medium high heat. Simmer until curry is thick, shaking pan occasionally. Remove from heat and add roasted curry powder, cover and let stand for flavors to blend until ready to serve. Serve with rice and mallun.

Fence Gourd In Mustard Curry Sauce

2 med. tender fence gourds (ridged gourd)
¼ c. onion, chopped
2 cloves garlic, chopped
Dash fresh peeled grated ginger
1sm. green chili, seeded and chopped
1 T. vegetable curry powder, page 196
2½ c. coconut milk or soymilk
1 T. country Dijon mustard
Salt to taste

Peel off thick skin and sharp edges of fence gourd. Wash under running cold water; pat dry with paper towels. Slice in 3/4 –inch rounds; do not remove center pulp with seeds. Transfer to nonstick shallow skillet. Add rest of the ingredients except salt to taste. On high heat, bring to boil; reduce to medium heat. Uncover and simmer until fence gourd is slightly tender. Add salt to taste; stir. Simmer until curry is slightly thick stirring occasionally. Remove from heat and serve with rice.

Jerusalem Artichokes In A Yellow Curry Sauce

1 lb. Jerusalem artichokes
¼ c. onion, chopped
2 cloves garlic, chopped
Dash fresh peeled grated ginger
1sm. green chili, seeded and chopped
1 med. tomato, chopped
1 T. vegetable curry powder, page 196
2½ c. coconut milk or soymilk
Lemon pepper to taste

Peel artichokes, removing any knobby bits. Slice and transfer to a bowl of water with 1 tablespoon lemon juice. Wash well and drain water. Combine rest of the ingredients in nonstick shallow skillet. Add the artichokes. On high heat, bring to a boil; reduce to medium heat. Cover and cook for 5 minutes. Uncover; simmer until curry is slightly thick, stirring occasionally.

Red Lentils In Red Curry Sauce

1 c. red lentils
1 T. olive oil or canola oil
¼ c. onion, chopped
1 med. tomato, chopped
2 cloves garlic, chopped
1 thin slice fresh ginger, peeled, crushed and minced
Dash mustard seeds
3 c. water or vegetable stock
1 c. tomato sauce
1 ½ T. paprika
1 T. roasted curry powder, page 198
Dash cayenne pepper
Lemon pepper to taste

Place lentils in a bowl; wash well 3 or 4 times. Drain water; set aside. Heat nonstick saucepan; add oil. On medium-high heat, sauté onions, tomatoes, garlic and ginger until slightly soft. Add mustard seeds. Sauté until they pop; add washed lentils and the rest of the ingredients except lemon pepper. On high heat, bring to a boil; reduce to medium heat. Cover and cook until lentils are tender to a soft consistency of running porridge, stirring occasionally. Discard any foam that floats on top. Uncover; add lemon pepper to taste. Simmer for 5 minutes. Serve over rice or pasta.

Carrot Stir-Fry

3 med. carrots, peeled and julienned
1 tsp. paprika
½ tsp. vegetable curry powder, page 196
1/3 c. water
Lemon pepper to taste
2 T. olive oil or canola oil
¼ c. onion, chopped
1 T. fresh parsley, chopped
Dash cayenne pepper

In nonstick skillet, combine carrots, paprika, vegetable curry powder and water. Add lemon pepper to taste. On high heat, bring to a boil. Reduce to medium heat. Cover and cook until carrots are tender; remove from heat. Transfer to a bowl; set aside. Return skillet to medium heat; add oil. Sauté onions and parsley for 2 minutes; add cooked carrots. Add cayenne pepper. Sauté until liquid is absorbed, stirring occasionally. Serve over rice.

Artichoke Carrot And Spinach In Yellow Curry Sauce

1 (14-oz.) can artichoke hearts, drained and rinsed
2 med. carrots, peeled and sliced diagonally
¼ c. onion, chopped
2 cloves garlic, chopped
Dash fresh peeled grated ginger
1 T. vegetable curry powder, page 196
2 c. coconut milk or soymilk
Lemon pepper to taste
2 c. fresh baby spinach

In nonstick shallow skillet, combine artichokes and rest of the ingredients except spinach. On high heat, bring to a boil; reduce to medium heat. Uncover and simmer until carrots are slightly tender, stirring occasionally. Add spinach and simmer until wilted. Remove from heat. Serve with rice.

Sauteed Cabbage

1 sm. head cabbage, washed and shredded
½ tsp. paprika
½ tsp. vegetable curry powder, page 196
Lemon pepper to taste
3 T. olive oil or vegetable oil
1 sm. onion, halved and finely sliced
Dash dry chili pepper flakes

In a bowl, combine shredded cabbage, paprika, vegetable curry powder and lemon pepper to taste. Mix well with hand to combine, set aside. Place nonstick shallow skillet on medium-high heat; add oil; heat and sauté onions for 2 minutes. Add combined cabbage; cover and cook 3 minutes. Uncover; add chili pepper flakes. Sauté until liquid is absorbed, stirring constantly. Remove from heat and serve with rice.

Sauteed Jicama

1 lg. tender jicama, peeled and julienned
1 tsp. vegetable curry powder, page 196
1 tsp. paprika
Lemon pepper to taste
3 T. olive oil
1 sm. onion, chopped
1sm. green chili, seeded and chopped
¼ c. fresh parsley, chopped
More lemon pepper if needed

In a bowl, combine jicama, vegetable curry powder and paprika. Add lemon pepper to taste; set aside. Place a nonstick shallow skillet on medium heat; add oil, heat and sauté onion and green chili. Add combined jicama; cover and cook 5 minutes. Uncover; add parsley. Sauté until liquid is absorbed, stirring constantly. Add more lemon pepper to taste if needed. Remove from heat and serve with rice.

Deviled Jackfruit With Onions, Tomatoes, Peppers And Leeks

1 (10-oz.) can green Jackfruit, drained and rinsed
3 T. olive oil or canola oil
1 banana pepper or jalapeno pepper, finely sliced diagonally
1 med. tomato diced
1 sm. onion, halved and sliced
1 T. paprika
Lemon pepper to taste
1 c. julienned leeks

Place Jackfruit in a small pan; cover with water ½ inch above. On high heat, bring to boil; reduce to medium heat. Cover and cook until slightly tender. Remove from heat; drain water. Set aside. Heat nonstick shallow skillet; add oil. On medium-high heat, sauté pepper, tomatoes and onions until slightly soft, stirring occasionally. Add jackfruit, paprika and lemon pepper to taste; add leeks and sauté, stirring constantly until liquid is absorbed. Serve over rice.

Cabbage Mallun

6 c. finely shredded cabbage (use dark green leaves)
¼ c. unsweetened shredded coconut
Dash turmeric powder
1/3 c. chopped red onion
Dash crushed red pepper flakes
Lime juice and salt to taste
Extra limejuice to taste, if needed

Combine all the ingredients except extra limejuice in a nonstick shallow skillet. Place skillet on medium heat, cover and cook until greens are slightly tender, stirring occasionally. Remove from heat; add extra limejuice to taste, if needed. Stir to combine; serve with rice and curry.

Note:
Do not overcook greens. Do not add water; cook with the water that clings to the leaves.

Kale Mallun

1 bunch of kale greens
1/3 c. unsweetened shredded coconut
Dash turmeric powder
1/3 c. red onion, chopped
1sm. green chili, seeded and chopped (opt.)
Lime juice and salt to taste
Extra limejuice, if needed

Discard spoiled and discolored kale leaves. Wash well to remove any sand; place in a colander to drain water. Shred kale finely; transfer to nonstick shallow skillet. Add rest of the ingredients except extra limejuice. Place skillet on medium heat, cook kale until liquid is absorbed, stirring constantly. Remove from heat; add extra lime juice, if needed. Stir to combine. Serve with rice and curry.

Note:
Do not overcook greens. Do not add water; cook with
water that clings to leaves.

Mango Pineapple Curry

2 med. semi-ripe firm mangos
1 sm. fresh ripe pineapple
¼ c. onion, chopped
2 cloves garlic, chopped
Dash fresh peeled grated ginger
2 T. paprika
2 T. roasted curry powder, page 198
½ tsp. cayenne pepper, (opt.)
2½ c. coconut milk
Salt to taste

Peel mangos and slice into large chunks. Do not discard seeds; set aside. Discard crown of pineapple; cut off skin. With point of knife, remove eyes from pineapple. Cut in half and then into quarters. Cut off core and discard. Cut pineapple into large chunks; set aside. Combine mango, including seeds, pineapple and rest of ingredients in a nonstick skillet. On high heat, bring to boil; reduce to medium heat. Cover and simmer until mango and pineapple is tender and curry is slightly thick, stirring occasionally.

Sauteed Onions

2 med. red onions, halved and finely sliced
1 sm. tomato, chopped
1sm. green chili, seeded and chopped
2 T. paprika
Lime juice salt and pepper to taste
2 T. olive oil or canola oil

Combine first 5 ingredients in a bowl. Mix with hand; set aside. Heat a nonstick skillet. On medium heat, add oil; sauté combined ingredients until onions are slightly soft. Reduce to low heat; cover and simmer until liquid is absorbed, stirring occasionally. Serve with roti or stuff inside pita bread.

Eggplant And Jackfruit In Curried Mustard Sauce

2 med. eggplants, halved and sliced diagonally
1 tsp. salt
1 (10-oz.) can young tender Jackfruit, drained and rinsed
¼ c. onion, chopped
2 cloves garlic, chopped
Dash fresh peeled grated ginger
1 T. paprika
1 tsp. vegetable curry powder, page 196
2½ c. water
Lemon pepper to taste
2½ c. coconut milk or soymilk
2 T. country Dijon mustard

Place sliced eggplant in a colander over a pan. Sprinkle with salt; let stand at least 20 minutes for bitter juices to drain. Rinse under cold running water; press with back of wooden spoon to drain excess water. In nonstick shallow skillet, combine eggplant, Jackfruit and rest of the ingredients except milk and mustard. On high heat, bring to a boil; reduce to medium heat. Cover and cook until vegetables are tender, stirring occasionally. Add milk and mustard; stir. Uncover and simmer until curry is slightly thick. Remove from heat and serve with rice.

Lentil Curry With Tofu

1 c. cooked lentils, page 88
¼ c. onion, chopped
2 cloves garlic, chopped
1 med. tomato, chopped
2 c. coconut milk or soymilk
1 (16-oz.) pkg. tofu, cut into 4 pieces
1 ½ T. paprika
¼ tsp. cayenne pepper
Lemon pepper to taste

In nonstick shallow skillet, combine cooked lentils, onion, garlic, tomato and milk. Stir to combine. Add rest of the ingredients; stir to combine. On high heat, bring to a boil; reduce to low heat. Cover and simmer until thick, stirring occasionally. Serve over rice or pasta.

Sauteed Beets And Greens

1 bunch tender beets with greens
1 T. paprika
2 T tomato paste
1 c. water
3 T. olive oil or vegetable oil
1 sm. onion, chopped
Dash dry chili pepper flakes
Lemon pepper to taste

Separate greens from beets; discard discolored and spoiled leaves and tough stems. Rinse a few times under cold running water to remove any sand. Place leaves over a colander to drain water. Pat dry leaves with paper towels. Scrub and rinse beets under running cold water. Peel beets, shred beets and greens, chop stems. Transfer to a nonstick shallow skillet; add paprika, tomato paste and water; stir to combine. On high heat, bring to a boil; reduce to medium heat. Cover and cook until water is absorbed, stirring occasionally. Remove from heat; transfer the cooked beets and greens to a bowl. Return skillet to medium heat. Add oil. Add onions and chili pepper flakes; add cooked beets and green. Add lemon pepper to taste. Sauté until liquid is absorbed, stirring constantly. Remove from heat and serve with rice.

Quick Easy Lentil Curry

1 c red lentils
2 c. water
¼ c. onion, chopped
2 cloves garlic, chopped
1 T. vegetable curry powder, page 196 or dash turmeric powder
1 c. coconut milk or soymilk
Lemon pepper to taste

In nonstick saucepan, combine lentils, water, onion, garlic and vegetable curry powder or turmeric. On high heat, bring to a boil; reduce to low heat. Cover and cook until lentils are soft, stirring occasionally. Discard any foam that floats on top. Add milk and lemon pepper to taste; stir to combine. Uncover and simmer until slightly thick, stirring occasionally.

Deviled Channa Dhal (Yellow Split Peas)

1 c. channa-dhal, soaked overnight, drained and washed well
2½ c. water
1 T. paprika
1 banana pepper or jalapeno pepper, seeded and finely sliced diagonally
1 c. cherry tomatoes, halved
1 sm. onion, sliced
Dash hot sauce
1 tsp. paprika
3 T. olive oil or canola oil
Lemon pepper to taste
1 c. chopped green onions

In nonstick saucepan, combine channa-dhal, water and paprika. On high heat, bring to a boil; reduce to medium heat. Cover and cook until just tender, stirring occasionally. Discard any foam that floats on top. Remove from heat; set aside. In a bowl, combine peppers, tomatoes, onion, hot sauce and paprika. Set aside. Heat nonstick shallow skillet; add oil. On medium-high heat, sauté combined ingredients 2 minutes; add cooked channa-dhal and stir. Add lemon pepper to taste; add green onions. Sauté until liquid is absorbed, stirring constantly. Remove from heat; serve over rice.

Spicy Lentil Curry

1 c. red lentils
2 c. water
1 T. paprika
½ tsp. cayenne pepper
1 tsp. roasted curry powder, page 198
2 T. olive oil or canola oil
¼ c. chopped onions
Dash curry leaves
3 sm. whole dried chili pepper
Dash mustard seeds
2½ c. coconut milk or soymilk
Salt and limejuice to taste

Wash lentils well 3 or 4 times; drain water. In a nonstick saucepan, combine lentils, water, paprika, pepper, cayenne pepper and roasted curry powder. On high heat, bring to a boil; reduce to low heat. Cover and cook until tender and water is absorbed, stirring occasionally. Discard any foam that floats on top. Remove from heat; transfer lentils to a bowl. Return saucepan to medium heat. Add oil and heat; sauté onions and curry leaves for 2 minutes. Add chili peppers and mustard seed. Sauté until mustard seeds pop. Quickly add the cooked lentils; sauté slightly. Add milk and stir. Add salt and lime juice to taste. Reduce to low heat; uncover and simmer until slightly thick. Serve over rice or pasta

Baked Eggplant

4 med. eggplant
2 tsp. salt
Oil for brushing

Trim eggplant; slice lengthwise into ½ -inch slices. Place in colander; sprinkle eggplant with salt on both sides. Set aside for 20 minutes. Rinse eggplant under cold running water; pat dry with paper towels. Lightly brush both sides with oil. Layer eggplant on lightly greased baking sheet; do not overcrowd. Bake eggplant at 400(F) degrees for 40 minutes (20 minutes on each side) until golden brown and just tender. Remove from oven; transfer to absorbent paper towels to drain any excess oil; let cool. Freeze in freezer bag to use in recipes.

Curried Tofu With Carrots

1 pkg. silken tofu (extra firm), drained and cut into thick slices
1 tsp. lemon pepper
3 c. coconut milk or soymilk
¼ c. onion, chopped
2 cloves garlic, chopped
Dash fresh peeled grated ginger
1 sm. green chili, seeded and minced
2 T. paprika
1 T. roasted curry powder, page 198
2 med. carrots, peeled and finely sliced

Place tofu in a shallow nonstick skillet, sprinkle lemon pepper over tofu. Add milk and rest of the ingredients. On high heat, bring to a boil; reduce to medium heat. Cover and cook for 5 minutes; uncover. Simmer until tofu has absorbed flavors and carrots is tender, shaking pan occasionally. Remove from heat. Serve over rice or pasta.

Sauteed Bean Sprouts

1 lb. fresh bean sprouts
1 T. paprika
Lemon pepper to taste
3 T. olive oil or canola oil
1 sm. red onion, finely sliced
1 sm. tomato, halved, seeded and chopped
Dash hot sauce
¼ c. fresh parsley, chopped

Rinse bean sprouts; pat dry with paper towels. Add paprika and lemon pepper to taste, set aside. On medium-high heat, place nonstick shallow skillet; add oil and heat, sauté onion and tomato until soft. Add combined bean sprouts; sauté until liquid is absorbed. Add hot sauce and parsley; sauté 2 minutes. Remove from heat and serve with rice.

Deviled Portobello Mushrooms With Cashew Nuts

2 med. firm Portobello mushrooms
3 T. olive oil or canola oil
1 banana pepper or jalapeno pepper; seeded and sliced diagonally
1 sm. red onion, sliced
1 med. tomato, diced
½ c. cashew nuts
1½ T. paprika
Dash hot sauce
Lemon pepper to taste

Using wet paper towel, clean mushrooms caps. Hold the mushrooms upright and carefully scrape off the gills with a small spoon. Cut into thick slices; set aside. Heat nonstick shallow skillet; add oil. On medium-high heat, sauté peppers, onion and tomato for 2 minutes. Add mushrooms and cashew nuts. Cover and cook for 2 minutes. Uncover; add paprika, hot sauce and lemon pepper. Sauté until liquid is absorbed, stirring constantly.

Ash Plantain Curry

4 med. ash plantains
¼ c. onion, chopped
2 cloves garlic, chopped
¼ tsp. ginger, minced
¼ tsp. fresh green chili, seeded and minced
Dash curry leaves, (opt.)
Dash turmeric powder
1½ c. water
Salt and limejuice to taste
2½ c. coconut milk or soymilk
Dash roasted curry powder, page 198

Peel ash plantains; slice diagonally. Transfer ash plantains to bowl of water with ½ teaspoon limejuice, drain water. In a nonstick shallow skillet, combine ash plantains and the rest of the ingredients except milk and roasted curry powder. On high heat, bring to a boil; reduce to medium heat. Cover and cook until water is absorbed, stirring occasionally. Add milk; stir. Uncover and simmer until curry is slightly thick. Remove from heat; sprinkle with dash of roasted curry powder. Cover and let stand for 5 minutes for flavors to blend. Serve over rice.

Mixed Mushroom Curry

½ lb. button mushrooms, cleaned and halved
½ lb. cremini mushrooms, cleaned and halved
½ lb. shiitake mushrooms, cleaned, trimmed and thickly sliced
¼ c. onion, chopped
2 cloves garlic, chopped
Dash fresh peeled grated ginger
1 sm. green chili, seeded and chopped
1 T. vegetable curry powder, page 196
2 c. coconut milk or soymilk
Lemon pepper to taste

Combine all the ingredients in a nonstick shallow skillet. On high heat bring to a boil. Reduce to medium heat. Uncover and simmer until slightly thick, stirring occasionally. Remove from heat and serve with rice or pasta.

Okra In Yellow Curry Sauce

1 lb. sm. tender fresh okra or 1 (16-oz) pkg. frozen okra, thawed
¼ c. onion, chopped
2 cloves garlic, chopped
Dash fresh peeled grated ginger
1 sm. green chili, seeded and chopped
2 c. coconut milk or soymilk
Dash turmeric powder
Salt to taste

Combine okra and the rest of the ingredients on high heat, bring to boil, reduce to medium heat. Uncover and simmer until okra is slightly tender, stirring occasionally.

Note:
If using fresh okra, clean okra using wet paper towel, do not cut off tops from fresh or frozen okra.

Sauteed Celery

1 bunch celery, washed and sliced, including leaves
1 T. paprika
Dash hot pepper sauce
3 T. olive oil or canola oil
1 sm. red onion, halved and finely sliced
1 med. tomato, chopped
1 sm. green chili, seeded and chopped
Lemon pepper to taste

Combine first 3 ingredients in a bowl, set aside. On medium-high heat, place nonstick shallow skillet. Add oil, heat and sauté onion, tomato and green chili for 3 minutes. Add combined celery. Sauté until slightly tender and liquid is absorbed, stirring constantly. Remove from heat. Serve with rice.

Spicy Lentil Curry With Artichokes

1 c. red lentils
2 c. water
1 T. paprika
½ tsp. cayenne pepper
1 T. olive oil or canola oil
¼ c. onions, chopped
2 cloves garlic, chopped
1 sm. whole dry chili pepper, broken in pieces
Dash mustard seeds
1 (14-oz.) can artichokes, drained and rinsed
1½ c. coconut milk or soymilk
Lemon pepper to taste

Wash lentils well 3 or 4 times; drain water. In a nonstick saucepan, combine lentils, water, paprika, cayenne pepper; stir. On high heat, bring to a boil; reduce to low heat. Cover and cook until lentils are soft. Remove from heat; set aside. Heat small nonstick skillet. On medium high heat add oil; sauté onion, garlic chili pepper and mustard seeds for 2 minutes, stirring constantly. Remove from heat and add to the cooked lentils. Return sauce pan with cooked lentils to medium heat; add artichokes and milk; stir. Uncover and simmer until slightly thick.

Carrots And Beans In Curry Sauce

2 med. carrots, peeled and sliced
½ lb. string beans, strings removed and cut into 1-in pieces
¼ c. onion, chopped
2 cloves garlic, chopped
1½ T. vegetable curry powder, page 196
1½ c. water
Lemon pepper to taste
2½ c. coconut milk or soymilk
Dash roasted curry powder, page 198

In nonstick shallow skillet, combine carrots and rest of the ingredients, except milk and roasted curry powder. On high heat, bring to a boil; reduce to medium heat. Cover and cook until water is absorbed, stirring occasionally. Add milk and stir. Uncover and simmer until curry is slightly thick. Remove from heat, sprinkle with dash of roasted curry powder. Cover and let stand 5 minutes for flavors to blend. Serve over rice

Fried Eggplant

4 med. eggplant
2 tsp. salt
Oil for frying

Trim eggplant; slice diagonally. Place in colander; sprinkle eggplant with salt on both sides. Set aside for ½ hour to drain out bitter juices Rinse eggplant under cold running water; pat dry with paper towels; set aside. Place deep fryer with oil on high heat; let oil bubble. Add eggplant and fry in batches until golden brown and slightly crispy; do not burn. Transfer to absorbent paper towels to drain any excess oil; let cool. Freeze in freezer bag to use in recipes.

Cashew Nut Curry With Spinach

2½ c. whole cashew nuts
¼ c. onion, chopped
2 cloves garlic, chopped
1 tsp. fresh green chili, seeded and chopped
1 thin slice fresh ginger, peeled, crushed and minced
1½ T. vegetable curry powder, page 196
2½ c. coconut milk or soymilk
Lemon pepper to taste
3 c. fresh baby spinach

In nonstick saucepan, combine cashew nuts and rest of the ingredients except spinach. On high heat, bring to a boil; reduce to medium heat. Uncover and cook until cashew nuts are just tender, stirring occasionally. Add spinach, simmer until wilted; stirring constantly. Remove from heat. Serve over rice.

Curried Okra in Red Mustard Sauce

1 lb. sm. fresh tender okra or 1 (16-oz) pkg. frozen okra, thawed
2 c. coconut milk or soymilk
¼ c. onion, chopped
2 cloves garlic, chopped
Dash fresh peeled grated ginger
2 T. paprika
1 tsp. roasted curry powder, page 198
2 T. country Dijon mustard
Salt to taste

Combine okra and rest of the ingredients in a nonstick shallow skillet on high heat. Bring to boil, reduce to medium heat. Uncover and simmer until okra is slightly tender, do not overcook.

Note:
If using fresh okra clean okra using wet paper towels, do not cut off tops of fresh or frozen okra.

Roasted Garlic With Spinach

3 c. roasted garlic, page 195
¼ c. onion, chopped
1 sm. green chili, seeded and chopped
2½ c. coconut milk or soymilk
Dash turmeric powder
Lemon pepper to taste
2-c. pkg. fresh baby spinach

In nonstick shallow skillet, combine garlic and rest of the ingredients except spinach. On high heat, bring to a boil; reduce to medium heat. Cover and cook for 5 minutes. Uncover; add spinach. Simmer until spinach is wilted and curry is slightly thick, stirring constantly.

Roasted Garlic Curry

3 c. roasted whole garlic cloves, page 195
¼ c. onion, chopped
1 sm. tomato, chopped
2 T. paprika
1 T. roasted curry powder, page 198
2 c. coconut milk or soymilk
Lemon pepper to taste

In small nonstick shallow skillet, combine garlic and rest of the ingredients. On high heat, bring to a boil. Reduce to low heat; cover and simmer until curry is thick, stirring occasionally.

Spicy Eggplant Curry

3 c. cooked eggplant, baked, fried, grilled or broiled
1½ c. coconut milk or soymilk
1 red onion, halved and finely sliced
1 thin slice fresh ginger, peeled, crushed and minced
2 cloves garlic, minced
1 T. paprika
1 ½ tsp. roasted curry powder, page 198
1 tsp. cayenne pepper
1 tsp. country Dijon mustard
Pinch sugar
¼ c. lime juice
Salt to taste

In nonstick shallow skillet, combine eggplant and rest of the ingredients. On high heat, bring to a boil. Reduce to low heat. Uncover and simmer until curry is thick, stirring occasionally.

Artichoke Hearts With Lentils In A Red Curry Sauce

1 (14-oz.) can artichoke hearts, drained and rinsed
1 c. cooked red lentils, page 88
¼ c. onion, chopped
2 cloves garlic, chopped
1½ T. paprika
1½ T. roasted curry powder, page 198
Dash cayenne pepper
2 c. coconut milk or soymilk
Lemon pepper to taste

In nonstick saucepan, combine artichokes and rest of the ingredients. On high heat, bring to a boil. Stir. Reduce to medium heat, cover and cook for 7 minutes. Uncover; simmer until curry is slightly thick.

Deviled Tofu

3 T. olive oil or canola oil
1 banana pepper or jalapeno pepper, seeded and sliced diagonally
1 med. tomato, diced
1 sm. onion, sliced
1 pkg. firm tofu, drained and cubed
1 T. paprika
Dash hot sauce
Lemon pepper to taste

Heat nonstick shallow skillet; add oil. On medium –high heat, sauté peppers, tomato and onion until slightly soft, stirring occasionally. Add tofu, paprika, hot sauce; add lemon pepper to taste. Sauté until liquid is absorbed, shaking pan occasionally.

Deviled Beets And Carrots

3 T. olive oil or vegetable oil
1 banana pepper or jalapeno pepper, seeded and sliced diagonally
1 med. tomato, diced
1 sm. onion, sliced
2 med. beets boiled, peeled and diced
2 med. carrots boiled, peeled and diced
1 T. paprika
¼ tsp. cayenne pepper (opt.)
Lemon pepper to taste
1 c. green onions, chopped

Place nonstick shallow skillet on medium heat; add oil and sauté pepper, tomato and onion until slightly soft. Add beets, carrots, paprika and cayenne pepper; sauté for 2 minutes. Add lemon pepper to taste and green onions. Sauté until liquid is absorbed, stirring constantly. Remove from heat; serve with rice.

Please see photo at back of book.

Mango Curry

4 semi-ripe mangoes
¼ c. onion, chopped
2 cloves garlic, chopped
1 thin slice fresh ginger, peeled, crushed and minced
2 T. paprika
1½ T. roasted curry powder, page 198
3 c. coconut milk or soymilk
Lemon pepper to taste

Peel mangoes and slice; discard seeds. Cut the sliced mango into large pieces. Combine mango and rest of the ingredients. On high heat, bring to boil; reduce to medium heat. Cover and cook until mango is soft and curry is thick, stirring occasionally.

Pineapple Curry

1 sm. fresh pineapple
¼ c. onion, chopped
2 cloves garlic, chopped
1 thin slice fresh ginger, peeled, crushed and minced
¼ c. fresh parsley
2 T paprika
1½ T. roasted curry powder, page 198
3 c. coconut milk or soymilk
Salt to taste

Discard crown of pineapple; cut off skin. With point of knife, remove eyes and discard. Cut pineapple in half and then into quarters. Cut off hard core and discard; cut pineapple into cubes. In a nonstick shallow skillet, combine pineapple and rest of the ingredients; stir. On high heat, bring to a boil; reduce to medium heat. Uncover and simmer until curry is thick, stirring occasionally. Serve over rice.

Sweet Potatoes With Spinach In A Yellow Curry Sauce

4 med. sweet potatoes, peeled and cut into sm. chunks
3 c. water
¼ c. onion, chopped
2 cloves garlic, chopped
1 thin slice fresh ginger, peeled, crushed and minced
1 T. vegetable curry powder, page 196
2½ c. coconut milk or soymilk
Lemon pepper to taste
2 c. fresh spinach

In nonstick saucepan, combine sweet potato, water, onion, garlic, ginger and vegetable curry powder. On high heat, bring to boil; reduce to medium heat. Cover and cook until slightly tender, stirring occasionally. Add milk and stir. Add lemon pepper to taste. Uncover; simmer until sauce is slightly thick, stirring occasionally. Add spinach; cover. Simmer until wilted. Serve over rice.

Artichoke Hearts With Spinach

1 (14-oz.) can artichoke hearts, drained and rinsed
¼ c. onion, chopped
2 cloves garlic, minced
1 thin slice fresh ginger, peeled, crushed and minced
1 T. vegetable curry powder, page 196
2 c. coconut milk or soymilk
Lemon pepper to taste
3 c. fresh spinach

In nonstick shallow skillet, combine artichokes and rest of the ingredients except spinach. On high heat, bring to a boil. Reduce to medium heat. Cover and cook for 10 minutes. Uncover; add spinach. Simmer until wilted, stirring occasionally.

Sauteed Spicy Artichoke Hearts

1 (14-oz.) can artichoke hearts, drained and rinsed
2 tsp. ginger soy sauce
1 tsp. cayenne pepper
Dash dry chili pepper flakes
1 T. lemon juice
2 T. canola oil or olive oil
1 sm. red onion, halved and finely sliced
1 c. cherry tomatoes, halved
1/3 c. fresh shredded basil

In a bowl, combine first 5 ingredients; set aside. On medium-high heat, place nonstick shallow skillet; add oil and heat. Sauté onions and tomatoes until soft; add combined artichokes. Sauté until liquid is absorbed, stirring constantly. Add shredded basil. Remove from heat; cover and let stand for 5 minutes for flavors to blend. Serve with rice.

Spicy Beet Root Curry

4 med. tender beets, peeled and cut into matchstick strips
¼ c. onion, chopped
1 tsp. chopped fresh garlic
Dash fresh grated ginger
1 T. paprika
1 ½ tsp cayenne pepper
1 tsp. seeded green chili, minced
1 c. water
Lemon pepper to taste
2 c. coconut milk or soymilk

In nonstick shallow skillet, combine beets and rest of the ingredients except milk. On high heat, bring to a boil; reduce to medium heat. Cover and cook until beets are slightly tender and water is absorbed, stirring occasionally. Uncover; add milk. Simmer until curry is thick. Remove from heat; serve with rice.

Beet Root Curry

4 med. tender beets, peeled and cut into matchstick strips
1½ c. water
¼ c. onion, chopped
2 cloves garlic, chopped
½ tsp. fresh green chili, seeded and chopped
1½ tsp. mild curry paste, page 196
Lemon pepper to taste
2 c. coconut milk or soymilk
2 T. fresh parsley, chopped

In nonstick shallow skillet, combine beets and rest of the ingredients except milk and parsley. On high heat, bring to boil; reduce to medium heat. Cover and cook until water is absorbed, stirring occasionally. Add milk and parsley. Stir. Uncover and Simmer until curry is thick, stirring occasionally.

Deviled Brussels Sprouts

½ lb. fresh Brussels sprouts, washed and halved
1 T. paprika
2 T. hot sauce
3 T. olive oil or vegetable oil
1 sm. onion, diced
1 sm. tomato, chopped
2 fresh green chili peppers, seeded and sliced diagonally
Lemon pepper to taste

Combine Brussels sprouts, paprika and hot sauce in a bowl; set aside. On medium heat, place nonstick shallow skillet; add oil. Sauté onion, tomato and green chilies 2 to 3 minutes; add combined Brussels sprouts. Add lemon pepper to taste. Sauté until liquid is absorbed, stirring constantly.

Brussels Sprout Curry

1 lb. fresh Brussels sprouts
¼ c. onion, chopped
2 cloves garlic, chopped
Dash fresh peeled grated ginger
1 sm. fresh chili pepper, seeded and chopped
1 med. tomato halved, seeded and chopped
2 T. paprika
1 T. roasted curry powder, page 198
2½ c. coconut milk or soymilk

Discard stems and discolored leaves; wash and drain water. Cut Brussels sprouts in halves; set aside. In nonstick shallow skillet, combine Brussels sprouts and rest of the ingredients; stir. On high heat, bring to a boil; reduce to medium heat. Cover and cook for 7 minutes. Uncover and simmer until curry is slightly thick, stirring occasionally. Remove from heat; serve with rice.

Pumpkin In Mustard Sauce

2½ lbs. pumpkin, (seeds and pulp removed and discarded)
¼ c. onion, chopped
2 cloves garlic, chopped
¼ tsp. fresh ginger, minced
Dash turmeric powder
2½ c. water
Lime juice and salt to taste
2½ c. coconut milk or soymilk
1 ½ T. country Dijon mustard

Scrub skin of pumpkin; wash well. Cut into small chunks, in nonstick shallow skillet, combine pumpkin and rest of the ingredients except milk and mustard. On high heat, bring to a boil; reduce to medium heat. Cover and cook until water is absorbed, stirring occasionally. Add milk and mustard; stir. Uncover and simmer until sauce is thick. Remove from heat; serve with rice.

Cooked Lentils

2 c. red lentils
4 c. water
Dash turmeric powder or vegetable curry powder, page 196
2 T. olive oil or canola oil
¼ c. onion, chopped
2 cloves garlic, chopped
1 thin slice fresh ginger, peeled crushed and minced
Dash curry leaves or sm. bay leaf
Dash mustard seeds
Salt to taste

Wash lentils well 3 or 4 times; drain water. In a nonstick saucepan, combine lentils, water, and turmeric or vegetable curry powder. On high heat, bring to a boil; reduce to low heat. Cover and cook until tender and water is absorbed, stirring occasionally. Discard any foam that floats on top. Remove from heat; set aside. Heat small nonstick skillet; add oil. On medium heat, sauté onion, garlic, ginger, curry leaves and mustard seeds stirring constantly until mustard seeds pop. Add to the cooked lentils and stir to combine. Return saucepan with cooked lentils to low heat; add salt to taste. Simmer until heated through, stirring constantly. Remove from heat; let cool. Freeze in freezer bags for use in recipes.

Deviled Artichoke Hearts

3 T. olive oil or canola oil
1 banana pepper or jalapeno pepper, seeded and sliced diagonally
1 med. tomato, diced
1 sm. onion, diced
1 (14-oz.) can artichoke hearts, drained and rinsed
1 T. paprika
Dash cayenne pepper
1 c. julienned leeks
Lemon pepper to taste

Heat nonstick shallow skillet; add oil. On medium-high heat, sauté peppers, tomatoes and onion until slightly soft. Add artichoke hearts; sauté 2 minutes. Add paprika, cayenne pepper and lemon pepper to taste; add leeks. Sauté until liquid is absorbed, stirring constantly.

Cooked Chickpeas

2 c. dried chickpeas
Water
Salt

Place dried chickpeas in a large pan. Wash few times; drain water. Cover with fresh water 6 inches above; soak overnight. Discard chickpeas that float on top, transfer to a colander and rinse chickpeas few times. Transfer chickpeas back to pan, cover with water 4 inches above. On high heat bring to a boil; reduce to medium heat. Cover and cook until tender, stirring occasionally. Discard any foam that floats on top. Add salt to taste, simmer 30 minutes. Remove from heat, set aside to cool. Freeze in freeze bags for use in recipes.

Note:
Same method for any dried bean.

Spicy Stir-fry Okra Sauteed With Onions And Dry Chili Flakes

3 T. olive oil or canola oil
1 med. onion, halved and finely sliced
1(16-oz) pkg. frozen whole okra, (thawed), or 1lb. sm. fresh tender okra
(Do not cut off okra tops)
Dash dry chili pepper flakes
Dash cayenne pepper
½ tsp. paprika
Lemon pepper to taste

Heat nonstick shallow skillet; add oil. On medium-high heat, sauté onion until slightly caramelized, stirring constantly. Add okra and rest of the ingredients. Cover and cook for 5 minutes or until slightly tender, stirring occasionally. Do not overcook.

Please see photo at back of book.

Red Lentils With Spinach In A Yellow Curry Sauce

1 c. red lentils
2 c. water
¼ c. onion, chopped
2 cloves garlic
1 thin slice fresh ginger, peeled and minced
1 T. vegetable curry powder, page 196
3 c. fresh spinach
2 c. coconut milk or soymilk
Lemon pepper to taste

Wash lentils well 3 or 4 times; drain water. In a nonstick saucepan, combine lentils, water, onion, garlic and vegetable curry powder; stir. On high heat, bring to a boil; reduce to medium heat. Cover and cook until lentils are tender, stirring occasionally. Discard any foam that floats on top. Add spinach and milk; stir. Add lemon pepper to taste. Reduce to low heat. Cover and simmer until spinach is wilted. Serve with rice.

Vegetable Stew

1 med. fresh leek, washed, trimmed and cut diagonally into 1 –in. pieces
(set aside)
2 med. potatoes, peeled and quartered
2 med. carrots, peeled and cut into 2 inch pieces
2 med. turnips, peeled and quartered
1 celery root, peeled and cut into chunks
1 bay leaf
3 cloves garlic, chopped
1 thin slice fresh ginger, peeled and chopped
Water to cover 4 in. above vegetables
Vinegar, salt and pepper to taste
2 T. butter or olive oil
2 T. all-purpose flour
1 red onion, halved and quartered
¼ c. fresh chopped parsley

In nonstick heavy saucepan, combine potatoes, carrots, turnips, celery root, bay leaf, garlic, ginger and water. Add vinegar, salt, and pepper to taste. On high heat, bring to a boil; reduce to medium heat. Cover and cook until vegetables are slightly tender, stirring occasionally. Remove from heat; strain cooking liquid to a bowl; set aside. Heat nonstick skillet. Add butter or oil. Sauté onion, parsley and leeks 2 minutes; add flour, stirring constantly. Add cooking liquid and stir. Transfer to the saucepan with cooked vegetables; uncover and simmer until sauce is slightly thick, stirring occasionally. Serve over rice.

Bittermelon Curry (Called Bittergourd)

2 med. tender bittermelons
¼ c. onion, chopped
2 cloves garlic chopped
1 sm. green chili, seeded and chopped
Dash fresh peeled grated ginger
2 med. ripe tomatoes, chopped
1 T. paprika
2½ c. coconut milk or soymilk
Lemon pepper to taste
Fresh limejuice to taste

Slice bittermelon in half lengthwise. Using a spoon, scrape out fibrous pulp and seeds; discard. Slice bittermelon diagonally; transfer to a bowl. Pour very hot water over to remove bitterness; drain water. Wash and rinse bittermelon a few times; squeeze out excess water. Transfer to a nonstick shallow skillet; combine with rest of the ingredients. On high heat, bring to a boil; reduce to medium heat. Cover and cook 10 minutes. Uncover and simmer until bittermelon is tender and curry is thick, stirring occasionally.

Note:
This vegetable is very good for diabetics.

Roasted Garlic In Yellow Curry Sauce

3 c. roasted whole garlic cloves, page 195
¼ c. onion, chopped
1 sm. tomato, chopped
2 T. vegetable curry powder, page 196
2 c. coconut milk or soymilk
Lemon pepper to taste

In a small, nonstick shallow skillet, combine garlic and rest of the ingredients. On high heat, bring to a boil; reduce to low heat. Cover and simmer until curry is thick, stirring occasionally.

Eggplant Curry

2 med. eggplants, sliced diagonally, (fried, baked, grilled or broiled)
1 sm. onion, halved and finely sliced
2 cloves garlic chopped
1 thin slice fresh ginger, peeled, crushed and minced
1 sm. green chili, seeded and chopped
1 tsp. country Dijon mustard
2 T. paprika
2 T. roasted curry powder, page 198
2 T. red wine vinegar
½ c. coconut milk or soymilk
Lime juice and salt to taste
Dash sugar

Combine eggplant and the rest of the ingredients; stir. On high heat, bring to a boil; reduce to low heat. Uncover and simmer until liquid has been absorbed and curry is thick, stirring occasionally. Remove from heat; serve with any rice dish.

Roasted Garlic With Cashew Nuts

2 c. roasted garlic, page 195
2 c. cashew nuts
¼ c. onion, chopped
1 med. tomato, chopped
2 tsp. parsley, chopped
2 T. vegetable curry powder, page 196
2½ c. coconut milk or soymilk
Lemon pepper to taste

In nonstick shallow skillet, combine garlic and rest of the ingredients. On high heat, bring to a boil; reduce to medium heat. Cover and cook until cashew nuts are tender and curry is slightly thick, stirring occasionally.

Yellow Lentil Curry With Yogurt

1 c. red lentils
2½ c. water
1 T. vegetable curry powder, page 196
Lemon pepper to taste
2 T. olive oil or canola oil
¼ c. onion, chopped
2 sm. whole dry chili peppers
Dash mustard seeds
½ c. plain yogurt

Wash lentils well 3 or 4 times; drain water. In a nonstick saucepan, combine lentils, water and vegetables curry powder; add lemon pepper to taste. On high heat, bring to a boil; reduce to medium heat. Cover and cook until lentils are tender, to a soft consistency of running porridge, stirring occasionally. Discard any foam that floats on top. Remove from heat; transfer cooked lentils to a bowl. Return saucepan to medium-high heat. Add oil; sauté onions, chili and mustard seeds. Sauté until mustard seeds pop. Add cooked lentils; sauté slightly. Add yogurt. Stirring occasionally, simmer until heated through. Serve with rice.

Bell Pepper Stir-fry

1 med. red bell pepper, seeded and julienned
1 med. green pepper, seeded and julienned
1 med. yellow pepper, seeded and julienned
1 med. onion, halved and finely sliced
1 sm. green chili, seeded and chopped
2 T. chili sauce
Lemon pepper to taste
3 T. olive oil or canola oil
¼ c. fresh basil, chopped

In a bowl, combine first 7 ingredients; set aside. Heat oil in a nonstick skillet. On high heat, stir-fry the combined ingredients until liquid is absorbed and peppers are slightly tender, stirring constantly. Add fresh basil; toss. Remove from heat; cover and let stand, to allow flavors to blend.

Collard Green Mallun

1 bunch collard greens
½ c. unsweetened shredded coconut
Dash turmeric powder
1/3 c. red onion, chopped
1 sm. green chili, seeded and chopped (opt.)
Lemon pepper to taste
Fresh lime juice to taste

Discard spoiled and discolored leaves. Wash well to remove any sand. Place in colander to drain water. Shred collard greens finely; transfer to nonstick shallow skillet. Add rest of the ingredients except limejuice to taste. Place skillet on medium heat, cook collard greens until liquid is absorbed, stirring constantly. Remove from heat; add limejuice to taste. Stir to combine; serve with rice and curry.

Note:
Do not overcook greens. Do not add water; cook with
water that clings to leaves.

Boiled Chickpeas, Soy Beans Or Any Kind Of Beans

2 c. dried peas or beans
Salt to taste
water

Place dried peas or beans in a large pan. Discard any stones; wash a few times and drain. Pour fresh water to cover 6 inches above beans; soak overnight. Discard any skins or spoiled peas or beans that float on top. Drain water; pour fresh water to cover 4 inches above. On high heat, bring to a boil. Reduce to medium heat; cover and cook until tender, stirring occasionally. Discard any foam that floats on top. Add salt to taste. Reduce to low heat; cover and simmer for 10 minutes. Remove from heat; let cool. Transfer to a colander to drain water. Transfer to freezer bags; freeze for use in recipes.

Deviled Chickpeas

2 T. olive oil or canola oil
1 med. onion, halved and finely sliced
1 med. tomato, chopped
1 banana pepper or jalapeno pepper, sliced diagonally
Dash of mustard seeds
2 c. boiled chickpeas, page 97
Dash cayenne pepper
½ tsp. paprika
Lemon pepper to taste

Heat nonstick shallow skillet on medium-high heat; add oil and sauté onion, tomato and peppers until slightly soft. Add mustard seeds. Sauté until they pop; add chickpeas, cayenne pepper and paprika, stirring constantly. Add lemon pepper to taste. Sauté 2 to 3 minutes or until liquid is absorbed.

Curried Jackfriut

1 (10-oz.) can green Jackfruit, drained and rinsed or fresh tender
Jackfruit, on page 218
¼ c. onion, chopped
2 cloves garlic minced
1 slice fresh ginger, peeled and minced
1 med. tomato, chopped
1T. roasted curry powder, page 198
1½ tsp. paprika
Dash cayenne pepper
2½ c. coconut milk or soymilk
Lemon pepper to taste

In nonstick shallow skillet, combine all the ingredients. On high heat, bring to boil; reduce to medium heat; cover and cook until Jackfruit is slightly tender, stirring occasionally. Uncover; simmer until sauce is slightly thick.

Deviled Soybeans

2 T. olive oil or canola oil
1 med. onion, halved and finely sliced
1 med. tomato, chopped
1 banana pepper or jalapeno pepper, sliced diagonally
Dash of mustard seeds
Dash dry red pepper flakes
2 c. boiled soybeans, page 97
1 tsp. paprika
Lemon pepper to taste

Heat nonstick shallow skillet on medium-high heat; add oil. Sauté onions, tomatoes and peppers until slightly soft; add mustard seeds, sauté until they pop. Add pepper flakes, soybeans and paprika, stirring constantly. Add lemon pepper to taste; sauté 3 minutes or until liquid is absorbed. Serve over rice.

Artichoke Hearts In A Yellow Curry Sauce

1 (14-oz.) can artichoke hearts, drained and rinsed
¼ c. chopped onion
2 cloves garlic chopped
1 tsp. fresh green chili, seeded and minced
1 thin slice ginger, peeled and minced
1 med. tomato, chopped
1 ½ tsp. vegetable curry powder, page 196
Few curry leaves, (opt.)
1½ c. coconut milk or soymilk
Lemon pepper to taste

In a nonstick shallow skillet, combine artichokes and rest of the ingredients. Stir. On high heat, bring to a boil; reduce to medium heat. Cover and cook 7 minutes. Uncover; simmer until curry is slightly thick, stirring occasionally. Remove from heat; serve over rice.

Soybeans In Yellow Curry Sauce

2 c. cooked soybeans, page 97
2½ c. coconut milk or soymilk
¼ c. onion, chopped
2 cloves garlic chopped
Dash fresh peeled grated ginger
1 med. tomato, chopped
1 sm. green chili, seeded and chopped
1 T. vegetable curry powder, page 196 or ¼ tsp turmeric powder
Lemon pepper to taste

Combine all ingredients in a nonstick shallow skillet; stir. On high heat, bring to a boil; reduce to medium heat. Uncover and simmer until curry is slightly thick, stirring occasionally. Remove from heat; serve over rice or pasta.

Cashew Nuts In Yellow Curry Sauce

2½ c. fresh raw cashew nuts
¼ c. onion, chopped
2 cloves garlic chopped
Dash fresh peeled grated ginger
1 sm. green chili, seeded and chopped
2 T. vegetable curry powder, page 196 or ¼ tsp turmeric powder
2½ c. coconut milk or soymilk
Lemon pepper to taste
1 tsp. roasted curry powder, page 198

Combine cashew nuts and rest of the ingredients except roasted curry powder. On high heat, bring to a boil; reduce to medium heat. Uncover and simmer until cashew nuts are tender, stirring occasionally. Remove from heat; add roasted curry powder. Cover and let stand to allow flavors to blend. Serve with rice.

Tofu Curry With Fresh Baby Spinach

1 pkg. silken tofu (extra firm), drained and cut into thick slices
1 tsp. lemon pepper
¼ c. onion, chopped
2 cloves garlic chopped
Dash fresh peeled grated ginger
2 T. vegetable curry powder, page 196
2 c. coconut milk or soymilk
3 c. fresh baby spinach

Place tofu in nonstick shallow skillet, sprinkle lemon pepper over tofu; add rest of the ingredients. On high heat, bring to a boil. Reduce to medium heat. Cover and cook for 7 minutes. Uncover and simmer until curry is slightly thick, shaking pan occasionally. Remove from heat; serve over rice or pasta.

Please see photo at back of book.

Pumpkin With Fresh Spinach

2 lbs. pumpkin, peeled, seeded and cut into med. chunks
¼ c. onion, chopped
2 cloves garlic, chopped
1 sm. green chili, seeded and chopped
2 T. vegetable curry powder, page 196
2 c. water
Lemon pepper to taste
2½ c. coconut milk or soymilk
3 c. fresh baby spinach

In nonstick shallow skillet, combine pumpkin and rest of the ingredients except milk and spinach. On high heat, bring to a boil; reduce to medium heat. Cover and cook until pumpkin is slightly tender and water is absorbed, stirring occasionally. Add milk and spinach; uncover and simmer until spinach is wilted and curry is slightly thick, stirring occasionally. Remove from heat; serve over rice.

All In One Jack Pot

1 (10 –oz.) can green Jackfruit, drained and rinsed or fresh tender jackfruit
2 med. potatoes, cubed
1 c. cooked chickpeas, page 89
¼ c. onion, chopped
2 cloves garlic, minced
1 thin slice fresh ginger, peeled and minced
1 tsp. roasted curry powder, page 198
1 T. paprika
2 c. water
Lemon pepper to taste
1 ½ c. coconut milk or soymilk

In nonstick shallow skillet, combine all the ingredients except coconut milk or soymilk. On high heat, bring to a boil; reduce to medium heat. Cover and cook until potatoes are tender. Add coconut milk or soymilk; cover and simmer until sauce is slightly thick, stirring occasionally. Serve with rice.

Banana Blossom Curry

1 med. banana blossom
2 T. olive oil or canola oil
1 sm. onion, halved and finely sliced
2 med. tomatoes, chopped
2 cloves garlic, chopped
1 tsp. country Dijon mustard
1 ½ tsp. paprika
1 ½ c. coconut milk or soymilk
Lemon pepper to taste

Discard matured petals from blossom; cut in half. Discard stem. Slice blossom finely; transfer to a bowl of salted water. Let stand 10 minutes. Transfer to a colander to drain water, pressing with the back of spoon. Heat a nonstick shallow skillet. On medium-high heat, add oil; sauté onion, tomato, garlic and sliced blossom, stirring constantly for 5 minutes. Add mustard, paprika, milk and lemon pepper to taste; stir. On high heat, bring to a boil. Uncover and simmer until thick, stirring occasionally. Serve with rice.

Spicy Deviled Sweet Potato

3 med. sweet potatoes boiled, peeled and sliced
1 ½ T. paprika
Dash hot pepper sauce
3 T. olive oil or canola oil
1 sm. banana pepper or jalapeno pepper, sliced diagonally
1 med. tomato, diced
1 sm. onion, diced
1 c. julienned green onions
Lemon pepper to taste

In a bowl, combine sweet potato, paprika and hot pepper sauce; set aside. Heat nonstick shallow skillet; add oil. On medium heat, sauté pepper, tomatoes and onions until slightly soft; add combined sweet potatoes. Stir. Add lemon pepper to taste. Add green onions. Sauté stirring constantly until heated through.

Curried Cabbage

1 med. head of cabbage
¼ c. onion, chopped
2 cloves garlic, chopped
Dash fresh peeled ginger, grated
1 sm. green chili, seeded and chopped
1 T. vegetable curry powder, page 196
2½ c. coconut milk or soymilk
Lemon pepper to taste
½ tsp. roasted curry powder, page 198

Wash cabbage; cut into quarters. Cut off core and slice cabbage; set aside. In nonstick shallow skillet, combine cabbage and rest of the ingredients except roasted curry powder. On high heat, bring to a boil; reduce to medium heat. Uncover and simmer until cabbage is tender and curry is thick, stirring occasionally. Remove from heat; sprinkle with roasted curry powder. Cover and let stand 5 minutes to allow flavors to blend. Serve with rice.

Jicama In Yellow Mustard Curry Sauce

2 med. tender jicama, peeled and diced
¼ c. onion, chopped
2 cloves garlic, chopped
Dash fresh peeled ginger, grated
1 sm. green chili, seeded and chopped
1 T. vegetable curry powder, page 196
2 c. coconut milk or soymilk
Lemon pepper to taste
2 T. country Dijon mustard

In nonstick shallow skillet, combine jicama and rest of the ingredients except mustard. On high heat, bring to a boil; reduce to medium heat. Cover and cook 5 minutes. Uncover; stir. Add mustard. Simmer until jicama is tender and curry is slightly thick, stirring occasionally. Serve with rice.

Tofu Curry

1 (16-oz.) pkg. tofu, drained and sliced thick
Dash lemon pepper
1 ½ T. paprika
1½ T. roasted curry powder, page 198
¼ c. onion, chopped
2 cloves garlic, minced
1 thin slice fresh ginger, peeled, crushed and minced
¼ tsp. minced fresh chili pepper, (opt.)
Dash curry leaves, (opt.)
2 c. coconut milk or soymilk
More lemon pepper to taste, if desired

Place tofu in a nonstick shallow skillet, sprinkle dash of lemon pepper over tofu. Add rest of the ingredients except more lemon pepper to taste. On high heat, bring to a boil; reduce to medium heat. Cover and cook for 5 minutes. Uncover; stir. Add more lemon pepper to taste if desired. Simmer until sauce is slightly thick, shaking skillet occasionally.

Spicy Tofu Curry

1 (16-oz.) pkg. tofu, drained and sliced thick
Dash lemon pepper
¼ c. onion, chopped
2 cloves garlic, chopped
Dash fresh peeled ginger, grated
Pinch curry leaves, (opt.)
2 T. paprika
1 tsp. cayenne pepper
2 c. coconut milk or soymilk
More lemon pepper to taste, if desired

Place tofu in a nonstick shallow skillet, sprinkle dash of lemon pepper over tofu slices. Add rest of the ingredients except more lemon pepper to taste. On high heat bring to a boil; reduce to medium heat. Cover and cook for 5 minutes. Uncover and stir. Add more lemon pepper to taste if desired. Simmer until sauce is slightly thick, shaking skillet occasionally. Serve with rice or pasta.

Tofu Curry In Yellow Sauce

1 (16-oz.) pkg. tofu, drained and sliced thick
Dash lemon pepper
1½ tsp. vegetable curry powder, page 196
¼ c. onion, chopped
2 cloves garlic, chopped
1 thin slice fresh ginger, peeled, crushed and minced
¼ tsp. fresh green chili, seeded and minced
Dash curry leaves, opt
2½ c. coconut milk or soymilk
More lemon pepper to taste, if desired

Place tofu in a nonstick shallow skillet, sprinkle dash of lemon pepper over tofu slices. Add rest of the ingredients except more lemon pepper to taste. On high heat bring to a boil; reduce to medium heat. Cover and cook for 5 minutes. Uncover and stir. Add more lemon pepper to taste. Simmer until sauce is slightly thick, shaking skillet occasionally.

Eggplant And Cashew Nuts In Mustard Curry Sauce

2 c. cooked eggplant, (fried, baked, grilled or broiled)
1 c. cashew nuts
½ c. onion, chopped
2 cloves garlic, minced
1 thin slice fresh ginger, peeled, crushed and minced
½ tsp. fresh green chili, seeded and chopped
½ tsp. vegetable curry powder, page 196
1½ tsp. country Dijon mustard
1½ c. coconut milk or soymilk
Lime juice and salt to taste

In nonstick shallow skillet, combine eggplant and rest of the ingredients. On high heat, bring to a boil; reduce to medium heat. Uncover and cook until cashew nuts are tender and curry is thick, stirring occasionally.

Curried Cauliflower

1 med. head fresh cauliflower
¼ c. onion, chopped
1 tsp minced, garlic
Dash fresh grated ginger
Dash curry leaves, (opt.)
1 tsp. fresh green chili, seeded and chopped
2 T. paprika
1½ T. roasted curry powder, page 198
2 c. coconut milk or soymilk
Lemon pepper to taste

Wash cauliflower; cut off woody stems and discard. Separate cauliflower into florets. Slice tender stems. In nonstick shallow skillet, combine cauliflower and rest of the ingredients. On high heat, bring to a boil; reduce to medium heat. Cover and simmer until cauliflower is slightly tender and curry is slightly thick, stirring occasionally. Remove from heat; serve with rice.

Butternut Squash Curry

2 ½ lbs. butternut squash, peeled, seeded and cut into sm. chunks
¼ c. onion, chopped
2 cloves garlic, minced
¼ tsp. thin slice fresh ginger, minced
¼ tsp. fresh green chili, seeded and minced
Dash curry leaves, (opt.)
2 T. paprika
2 T. roasted curry powder, page 198
2 c. water
Lemon pepper to taste
2½ c. coconut milk or soymilk

In nonstick shallow skillet, combine butternut squash and rest of the ingredients except milk. On high heat, bring to a boil; reduce to medium heat. Cover and cook until water is absorbed, stirring occasionally. Add milk; stir. Uncover and simmer until curry is thick, stirring occasionally. Remove from heat; serve with rice or pasta.

Potatoes, Carrots And Spinach In Yellow Curry Sauce

2 med. potatoes, peeled and cut into sm. chunks
2 med. carrots, peeled and sliced diagonally
¼ c. onion, chopped
2 cloves garlic, minced
1 tomato, chopped
2 T. vegetable curry powder, page 196
2½ c. water
Salt to taste
2½ c. coconut milk or soymilk
3 c. fresh spinach
Lemon pepper to taste

In nonstick shallow skillet, combine potatoes and rest of the ingredients except milk, spinach and lemon pepper to taste. On high heat, bring to a boil; reduce to medium heat. Cover and cook until water is absorbed, stirring occasionally. Add milk, spinach, and lemon pepper to taste; uncover and simmer until curry is slightly thick and spinach is wilted, stirring occasionally. Remove from heat; serve with rice or pasta.

Sweet Potato With Eggplant

2 med. Fresh & tender eggplants cubed into 1 inch thick pieces
1 T. lemon pepper
3 T. olive oil
Preheat oven to 475 degrees (F).

Place eggplant cubes on a baking sheet, sprinkle with lemon pepper. Drizzle with olive oil and toss to coat. Spread them in a single layer and roast for 30 minutes, turning once or twice until golden brown.

For curry:

Roasted eggplant
½ red onion, finely chopped
1 green chili seeded & chopped
1 tsp. garlic, minced
½ tsp. minced ginger
1 T. roasted curry powder
1 T. chili powder
¼ c. white vinegar
½ c. coconut milk
dash of sugar
Salt to taste

In a nonstick skillet combine all the ingredients and stir well over high heat. Bring to a boil, reduce to low heat, cover and cook 5 minutes. Uncover and continue to simmer until the eggplant has absorbed the sauce, stirring occasionally. Remove from heat set aside.

2 med. sweet potato, boiled, peeled and cut into large cubes
2 T. olive oil
1 red bell pepper, seeded and diced
1 sm. onion diced
Few cherry tomatoes, halved
2 T. chili paste or chili sauce

Heat oil in shallow non-stick skillet over med: high heat. Add the sweet potato and sauté. Add rest of the ingredients and cooked eggplant curry. Stir to combine, simmer until sauce is absorbed stirring constantly. Remove from heat serve over rice.

Please see photo at back of book.

Soups

Curried Sweet Potato Soup

2 lg. sweet potatoes, peeled and sliced
8 c. water or stock
1 sm. onion chopped
1 stalk celery, sliced
6 cloves roasted garlic, page 195
1 tsp. Italian seasoning
½ tsp vegetable curry powder, page 196
1 bay leaf
1 tsp. roasted curry powder, page 198
Lemon pepper to taste
¼ c. fresh chopped chives

In a nonstick saucepan, combine first 9 ingredients. On high heat, bring to a boil. Reduce to medium heat; cover and cook until sweet potatoes are tender. Remove from heat, let cool. Discard bay leaf. Transfer soup to a blender or food processor. Blend to a smooth puree. Pour puree back into saucepan. If too thick, thin soup by adding more water or stock. Add lemon pepper to taste. Stir. Reheat for 5 minutes, stirring constantly. Ladle soup into bowls; garnish with chopped chives.

Curried Broth With Whole Roasted Garlic Cloves

2 whole garlic heads, roasted and peeled
1 (10 ½ -oz.) can low-sodium vegetable broth
1 c. water
½ tsp. roasted curry powder, page 198
Lemon pepper to taste
¼ c. green onions, chopped

In nonstick saucepan, combine all the ingredients except green onions. On high heat, bring to a boil; reduce to medium heat. Cover and cook for 12 minutes. Remove from heat; ladle soup into bowls. Garnish with green onions.

Vegetable Broth With Artichokes

1 (10½-oz.) can low-sodium vegetable broth
1 c. water
1 sm. red onion, halved and finely sliced
2 cloves garlic, minced
1 med. tomato, halved, seeded and chopped
¼ tsp. fresh minced thyme
1 tsp. roasted curry powder, page 198
1 (14-oz.) can artichokes, drained, rinsed and chopped
Lemon pepper to taste

In nonstick saucepan, combine all the ingredients except artichokes and lemon pepper to taste. On high heat, bring to a boil; reduce to medium heat. Cover and cook for 10 minutes. Uncover; add artichokes and lemon pepper to taste; cook 8 minutes. Serve hot.

Vegetable Soup

12 c. water
1/3 c. pearl barley
1 sm. onion chopped
2 cloves garlic, chopped
1 tsp. thin slice fresh ginger, peeled and minced
2 med. tomatoes, chopped
1 stalk celery, chopped
1 tsp. vegetable curry powder, page 196
1 med. carrot, peeled and sliced
1 c. fresh green beans, cut into 1-in. pieces
1½ c. cauliflower florets
1½ c. broccoli florets
1 med. zucchini, sliced
1 bay leaf
1 tsp. dried Italian seasoning
Lemon pepper to taste

In nonstick saucepan, combine first 8 ingredients. On high heat, bring to a boil. Reduce to medium heat, cover and cook until barley is tender, stirring occasionally. Add rest of the ingredients, cover and simmer until vegetables are tender, stirring occasionally. Uncover; stir. Remove from heat; ladle soup into bowls and serve hot with crusty bread.

Tamarind Pepper Broth

2 T. tamarind liquid
8 c. water
1 med. onion chopped
4 cloves garlic, crushed
1 thin slice fresh ginger, peeled and crushed
1 (1-in.) stick cinnamon
1 piece lemon grass
Dash cardamom pods
1 T. peppercorns
1 T. paprika
1 tsp. roasted curry powder, page 198
Bouquet garni
Salt, limejuice and pepper to taste

In nonstick saucepan, combine all ingredients except lime juice, salt and pepper to taste. On high heat, bring to a boil; reduce to medium heat; Cover and simmer for 20minutes; uncover. Add salt, lime juice and pepper to taste. Remove from heat; let cool. Strain broth. Pour into containers; freeze for use in soups.

Vegetable Broth With Portobello Mushrooms

2 med. Portobello mushrooms
1 (10½ -oz.) can low-sodium vegetable broth
3 c. water
6 shallots, peeled and finely sliced
2 cloves garlic, minced
1 thin slice fresh ginger, peeled and finely minced
1 med. tomato, halved, seeded and chopped
1 tsp. roasted curry powder, page 198
Lemon pepper to taste
¼ c. fresh parsley, chopped

Using wet paper towels, clean mushrooms caps. Hold upright and use a brush to cleanout any dirt from gills. Carefully trim stems and chop. Slice mushrooms and set aside. In a saucepan, combine chopped mushroom stems and rest of the ingredients except lemon pepper, parsley and sliced mushrooms. On high heat, bring to a boil. Reduce to medium heat; cover and cook for12 minutes. Uncover and add sliced mushrooms. Cover and cook 8 minutes. Remove from heat. Add lime juice to taste. Ladle into soup bowls; garnish with parsley.

Curried Parsnip And Potato Soup

1 lb. parsnips, peeled and sliced
4 med. potatoes, peeled and sliced
1 sm. onion, chopped
2 cloves garlic, chopped
1 thin slice fresh ginger, peeled and finely minced
1 stalk celery, sliced with leaves
1 bay leaf
½ tsp. dried basil
8 c. vegetable stock or water
1 tsp. roasted curry powder, page 198
Lemon pepper to taste
¼ c. fresh chopped chives for garnish

In nonstick saucepan, combine all ingredients except chopped chives. On high heat, bring to a boil; reduce to medium heat; cover and cook until parsnips and potatoes are tender, stirring occasionally. Remove from heat and discard bay leaf. Let it cool slightly. Transfer soup to blender; puree in batches. Return puree to saucepan. If too thick, thin soup by adding more stock or water. Reheat. Ladle soup into bowls; garnish with chives.

Curried Carrot Soup

1 lb. carrots, peeled and sliced
2 med. sweet potatoes, peeled and sliced
1 sm. onion, chopped
2 cloves garlic, chopped
Dash fresh peeled grated ginger
1 c. celery, sliced
1 bay leaf
Dash dried Italian seasoning
1 tsp. vegetable curry powder, page 196
8 c. water or stock
Lemon pepper to taste
Yogurt with dash of roasted curry powder, page 198 for garnish

In nonstick saucepan, combine all ingredients except yogurt and roasted curry powder for garnish. On high heat, bring to a boil; reduce to medium heat. Cover and cook until vegetables are tender, stirring occasionally. Remove from heat and discard bay leaf. Cool soup slightly; transfer soup to blender; puree in batches; return puree to saucepan. If soup is too thick, thin soup with more stock or water. Reheat soup, stirring constantly. Ladle soup into bowls; garnish with yogurt and sprinkle with roasted curry powder.

Broth With Bamboo Shoots

1 (10½ -oz.) can low-sodium vegetable broth
2 c. water
1 sm. onion, chopped
1 med. tomato, chopped
2 cloves garlic, chopped
1 thin slice fresh ginger, crushed and minced
1 tsp. roasted curry powder, page 198
½ tsp. dried Italian seasoning
1 (8-oz.) can bamboo shoots, drained and rinsed
Lemon pepper to taste

In nonstick saucepan, combine all ingredients except bamboo shoots and lemon pepper. On high heat, bring to a boil. Reduce to medium heat; cook 2 minutes. Add bamboo shoots and lemon pepper to taste. Cook 5 minutes. Remove from heat and serve hot.

Cream Of Roasted Tomato Soup

4 lg. firm ripe tomatoes
8 cloves roasted garlic
1 sm. onion, chopped
1 thin slice fresh ginger, peeled and chopped
1 tsp. roasted curry powder, page 198
Dash dried chili flakes
1 tsp. dried basil
8 c. vegetable stock
1 c. buttermilk or soymilk
Lemon pepper to taste
1/3 c. fresh shredded basil

Char tomatoes over gas flames, holding with tongs, turning tomatoes until blistered and charred on all sides, or char under broiler. Transfer tomatoes immediately to a paper bag and seal. Let stand 10 minutes. To peel tomatoes use wet paper towel to remove tomato skins. Cut tomato in half, scoop out seeds and chop. In nonstick heavy saucepan, combine chopped tomatoes and rest of the ingredients except milk, lemon pepper and basil. On high heat, bring to a boil. Reduce to medium heat; cover and cook 25 minutes. Remove from heat; let cool slightly. Transfer soup to blender; puree in batches. Pour puree back to saucepan and stir in milk. Add lemon pepper to taste. Simmer until heated through. Remove from heat and ladle soup into bowls. Garnish with shredded basil.

Pumpkin Soup

2 to 3 lbs. fresh pumpkin, peeled, seeded and cut into chunks
1 sm. onion, chopped
Dash fresh peeled grated ginger
2 cloves garlic, chopped
2 c. celery, sliced (including leaves)
1 med. tomato, halved, seeded and chopped
1 tsp. vegetable curry powder, page 196
1 bay leaf
Dash Italian seasoning
8 c. water or stock
Lime juice and salt to taste
Roasted curry powder for garnish, page 198

In nonstick saucepan, combine pumpkin and rest of the ingredients except roasted curry powder. On high heat, bring to a boil. Reduce to medium heat, cover and cook until pumpkin is tender, stirring occasionally. Remove from heat; discard the bay leaf. Transfer soup to blender; puree in batches. Return puree to saucepan and reheat. Ladle soup into bowls. Garnish with dash of roasted curry powder and serve.

Cream Of Root Vegetable Soup

2 med. rutabagas, peeled and sliced
3 med. parsnips, peeled and sliced
2 med. carrots, peeled and sliced
1 med. celeriac (celery root), peeled and sliced
1 sm. onion, chopped
6 cloves roasted garlic
10 c vegetable stock, page 138
1 tsp. vegetable curry powder, page 196
1 tsp. dried Italian seasoning
1 bay leaf
1/3 c. chopped green onions for garnish

In nonstick saucepan combine all ingredients, except green onions. On high heat bring to a boil. Reduce to medium heat. Cover and cook until vegetables are tender, stirring occasionally. Remove from heat and discard bay leaf. Let cool slightly; transfer soup to blender. Puree in batches. Return puree to saucepan. If soup is too thick, thin it with more stock. Reheat soup for 5 minutes. Ladle soup into bowls. Garnish with green onions.

Cream Of Roasted Red Bell Pepper Soup

6 lg. firm red bell peppers
8 cloves roasted garlic
1 sm. onion chopped
1 thin slice fresh ginger, peeled and chopped
1 ripe red chili pepper, halved, seeded and minced
1 tsp. roasted curry powder, page 198
8 c. vegetable stock, page 138
1 c. buttermilk or soymilk
Lemon pepper to taste
¼ c. fresh parsley, chopped

Char bell peppers over gas flames, holding with tongs, turning peppers until blistered and charred on all sides, or char under broiler. Immediately transfer pepper to paper bag, close to seal. Let stand 10 minutes. To peel peppers; use wet paper towel to remove skins. Cut in half; discard cores, ribs and seeds. Dice peppers reserve ½ c for garnish. In nonstick saucepan, combine diced peppers and rest of the ingredients except milk, lemon pepper and parsley. On high heat, bring to a boil. Reduce to medium heat; cover and cook for 15 minutes. Remove from heat; let cool. Transfer soup to blender; puree in batches. Pour puree back to saucepan; stir in milk; add lemon pepper to taste. Reheat soup 3 to 4 minutes. Ladle soup into bowls; garnish with parsley and reserved diced peppers.

Curried Potato Soup

1lb. potatoes (Yukon Gold), peeled and thinly sliced
8 c. water or stock
1 sm. onion chopped
6 cloves roasted garlic
1 stalk celery sliced
1 tsp. Italian seasoning
½ tsp. paprika
1 tsp. roasted curry powder, page 198
1 bay leaf
Lemon pepper to taste
¼ c. fresh parsley, chopped

In nonstick saucepan, combine first 9 ingredients. On high heat, bring to a boil. Reduce to medium heat, cover and cook until potatoes are tender. Remove from heat; let cool. Discard bay leaf. Transfer soup to blender or food processor; blend to a smooth puree. Pour puree back in saucepan; if too thick, thin with water or stock. Add lemon pepper to taste; stir. Reheat for 5 minutes, stirring constantly. Ladle soup into bowls; garnish with parsley.

Vegetable Broth With Button Mushrooms

3 c. vegetable broth or tamarind pepper broth, page 120
1 c. water
1 tsp. lemon juice
1 tsp. hot pepper sauce
1 ½ c. freshly sliced button mushrooms
Dash roasted curry powder, page 198

In a small nonstick saucepan, combine broth, water, lemon juice and hot pepper sauce. On high heat, bring to a boil. Reduce to medium heat; cook for 5 minutes. Add mushrooms; cook 3 minutes. Add curry powder; remove from heat. Serve hot.

Curried Pumpkin Soup

2 lbs. fresh pumpkin, peeled and cut into chunks
1 sm. onion chopped
2 cloves garlic, chopped
1 thin slice fresh ginger, peeled and chopped
1 med. tomato, halved, seeded and chopped
1 stalk celery sliced (leaves included), chopped
1 T vegetable curry powder, page 196
8 c. stock or water
Lime juice and salt to taste
Roasted curry powder for garnish, page 198

In nonstick saucepan, combine pumpkin and rest of the ingredients except roasted curry powder for garnish. On high heat, bring to a boil; reduce to medium heat. Cover and cook until pumpkin is tender. Remove from heat; let cool slightly. Transfer soup to blender; blend in batches to a smooth puree. Pour puree to saucepan. If too thick, thin with more stock or water. Reheat. Ladle soup into bowls; garnish with dash of roasted curry powder.

Cream Of Pumpkin Soup With Swiss Chard

2 to 3 lbs. pumpkin, peeled seeded and cut into chunks
10 c. water or stock
1 sm. onion chopped
8 cloves roasted garlic
1 bay leaf
1 T. country Dijon mustard
1 T. vegetable curry powder, page 196
1 ½ c. soymilk or yogurt
Lemon pepper to taste
2 c. shredded Swiss chard

In nonstick saucepan, combine first 7 ingredients. On high heat, bring to a boil; reduce to medium heat. Cover and cook until pumpkin is tender. Remove from heat; let cool. Discard bay leaf; transfer soup to blender, blend to a smooth puree. Pour puree to saucepan; add soymilk or yogurt; stir. Add lemon pepper to taste. Add Swiss chard; simmer until wilted, stirring constantly. Remove from heat. Serve into bowls.

Black Bean Soup

2 c. black beans, soaked overnight, washed well and drained
8 c. water
1 ½ tsp. Cajun seasoning
1 sm. onion chopped
8 cloves roasted garlic
1 thin slice fresh ginger, peeled and minced
1 med. carrot, peeled and chopped
1 stalk celery with leaves, chopped
Dash Cajun hot pepper sauce to taste
Yogurt for garnish, if desired

In nonstick saucepan, combine soaked beans, water and Cajun seasoning. On high heat, bring to a boil; reduce to medium heat. Cover and cook until tender, stirring occasionally. Discard any foam that floats on top. Remove 2 cups cooked beans from pan, transfer into a bowl and set aside. Add rest of the ingredients to cooked remaining beans in pan except Cajun hot pepper sauce to taste and yogurt. On high heat, bring to a boil; reduce to low heat. Cover and simmer for ½ hour, stirring occasionally. Remove from heat; let cool slightly. Transfer soup to blender; blend in batches to a smooth puree. Pour puree to saucepan. If too thick, thin with more water. Return pan to heat; add reserved cooked beans. Add Cajun hot pepper sauce to taste; stir. Cover and simmer for 10 minutes or until heated through, stirring occasionally. Remove from heat; ladle soup into bowls; garnish with a dollop of yogurt if desired.

Brown Lentil Soup

2 c. brown lentils
8 c. water or vegetable stock
1 sm. red onion, chopped
2 cloves garlic, chopped
1 thin slice fresh ginger, peeled and minced
2 med. tomatoes, chopped
1 stalk celery with leaves, chopped
1 sm. carrot, peeled and chopped
½ c. tomato sauce
1 bay leaf
Dash peppercorns
1 tsp. roasted curry powder, page 198
1 tsp. paprika
½ tsp. tamarind liquid
Lime juice and salt to taste

Sort lentils; discard any stones. Wash lentils well, drain water. Transfer lentils to a nonstick saucepan. Add rest of the ingredients except lime juice and salt to taste. On high heat, bring to a boil. Reduce to medium heat. Cover and cook until tender, stirring occasionally. Discard any foam that floats on top. Uncover; add lime juice and salt to taste. Simmer until soup is slightly thick, to a soft consistency. If soup is too thick, thin with more water. Simmer until heated through. Serve with crusty bread or over rice.

Cream Of Butternut Squash Soup

2 ½ lbs. butternut squash, peeled, seeded and cut into chunks
8 c. water or stock
1 stalk celery with leaves, sliced
1 sm. onion chopped
8 cloves roasted garlic
1 bay leaf
1 tsp. dried basil
1 tsp. roasted curry powder, page 198
1 ½ c. soymilk or yogurt
Lemon pepper to taste
¼ c. shredded fresh basil for garnish.

In nonstick saucepan, combine first 8 ingredients. On high heat, bring to a boil. Reduce to medium heat, cover and cook until squash is tender. Remove from heat; discard bay leaf. Transfer soup to blender or food processor; blend to a smooth puree. Pour puree back into saucepan. Add soymilk or yogurt and stir. Add lemon pepper to taste. Reheat; ladle soup into bowls. Garnish with basil and serve.

Lentil Mulligutawny

2 T. olive oil or canola oil
1 sm. red onion, halved and finely sliced
4 cloves garlic, crushed and minced
1 thin-sliced fresh ginger, crushed and minced
Dash curry leaves or 1 bay leaf
1 ½ -in. stick cinnamon
Piece of lemongrass
Dash peppercorns
1 stalk celery with leaves, chopped
2 med. tomatoes, chopped
1 ½ tsp. roasted curry powder, page 198
1 tsp. paprika
1 tsp. tamarind liquid
1 ½ c. red lentils, washed well until water runs clear
10 to 12 c. water or stock
Salt to taste

Heat nonstick saucepan, add oil. On medium-high heat, sauté onion, garlic, ginger, curry leaves, cinnamon and lemongrass 3 minutes. Add rest of the ingredients; stir to combine. On high heat, bring to a boil; reduce to medium heat. Cover and cook for 30 minutes or until lentils are tender, stirring occasionally. Discard any foam that floats on top. Uncover and simmer, until soup is slightly thick. Remove from heat and ladle into bowls; serve.

Note:
Before serving discard bay leaf, cinnamon stick and
lemongrass.

Cream Of Potato Soup With Parsley

1½ lbs. potato (Yukon Gold), peeled and sliced
8 c. vegetable stock or water
1 sm. onion chopped
8 cloves roasted garlic
1 stalk celery with leaves, sliced
1 tsp. roasted curry powder, page 198
1 bay leaf
1 tsp. dried parsley
1 ½ c. soymilk or yogurt
Lemon pepper to taste
½ c. fresh chopped parsley

In nonstick saucepan, combine first 8 ingredients. On high heat, bring to a boil. Reduce to medium heat, cover and cook until potatoes are tender. Remove from heat; let cool. Discard bay leaf. Transfer soup to blender or food processor; blend to a smooth puree. Pour puree back into saucepan. Add soymilk or yogurt and stir. Add lemon pepper to taste. Reheat stirring constantly, for 5 minutes. Remove from heat; ladle soup into bowls. Garnish with parsley.

Cream Of Sweet Potato Soup With Spinach

6 med. sweet potatoes, peeled and sliced
8 c. stock or water
1 stalk celery, sliced
1 sm. onion, chopped
8 cloves roasted garlic
1 tsp. roasted curry powder, page 198
1 bay leaf
1 tsp. Italian seasoning
1 ½ c. soymilk or yogurt
Lemon pepper to taste
2 c. fresh baby spinach

In nonstick saucepan, combine first 8 ingredients. On high heat, bring to a boil. Reduce to medium heat; cover and cook until potatoes are tender. Remove from heat; let cool. Discard bay leaf. Transfer soup to blender or food processor; blend to a smooth puree. Pour puree back into saucepan. Add soymilk or yogurt. Stir; add lemon pepper to taste. Add spinach; reheat until spinach wilts. Remove from heat; ladle soup into bowls and serve.

Vegetable Stock

2 T. olive oil or canola oil
1 sm. onion, diced
3 cloves garlic, crushed
1 thin-sliced fresh ginger, crushed
1 in. piece of lemongrass
1 med. leek, washed well trimmed and sliced
1 T. vegetable curry powder, page 196
4 qt. water (16 cups)
1 med. carrot, washed and sliced
1 sm. fennel bulb with fronds, sliced
1 med, tomato, halved seeded and diced
6 to 10 button mushrooms
1 celery stalk with leaves, chopped
Dash fennel seeds
20 peppercorns
10 cardamom pods
6 whole cloves
1 (1 –in.) stick cinnamon
Bouquet garni
Lemon pepper to taste

Heat nonstick heavy large saucepan on medium-high heat; add oil. Sauté onion, garlic, lemongrass, leeks and vegetable curry powder for 5 minutes, stirring constantly. Add water and the rest of the ingredients. On high heat, bring to a boil; reduce to medium heat. Cover and simmer for 1 hour, stirring occasionally. Season with more lemon pepper to taste, remove from heat; let cool. Line a large strainer with cheesecloth. Strain stock; pour into containers and freeze for use in recipes.

Tomato Soup With Cherry Pear Tomatoes

2 T. olive oil or canola oil
1 sm. red onion, chopped
3 med. tomatoes, chopped
3 cloves garlic, chopped
1 stalk celery with leaves, chopped
1 tsp. Italian seasoning
1 tsp. vegetable curry powder, page 196
1 bay leaf
8 c. water
2 (15-oz.) cans tomato sauce
2 c. fresh cherry pear tomatoes
1 med. red onion, halved and finely sliced
Lemon pepper to taste

Heat nonstick saucepan on medium-high heat; add oil heat and sauté onion, tomato, garlic, celery, Italian seasoning, vegetable curry powder and bay leaf for 5 minutes, stirring constantly. Add rest of the ingredients except sliced red onions and lemon pepper to taste. On high heat, bring to a boil. Reduce to medium heat. Cover and cook until tomatoes are soft. Uncover; add sliced onions and simmer 10 minutes, stirring occasionally. If the soup is thick, thin with more water; add lemon pepper to taste. Ladle soup into bowls; serve hot with crusty bread.

Curried Pumpkin Soup With Parsley

2 T. olive oil or canola oil
1 sm. onion, chopped
4 cloves garlic, minced
Dash fresh peeled ginger, crushed
1 ½ T. roasted curry powder, page 198
1 celery stalk with leaves, chopped
2 ½ lbs. pumpkin, peeled, seeded and cut into chunks
1 bay leaf
8 c. vegetable stock, page 138 or water
Lemon pepper to taste
1/3 c. fresh chopped parsley

Heat nonstick saucepan on medium heat; add oil, heat and sauté onion, garlic, ginger and curry powder 2 minutes. Add rest of the ingredients except parsley. On high heat, bring to a boil. Reduce to medium heat. Cover and cook until pumpkin is tender, stirring occasionally. Remove from heat. Let cool. Discard bay leaf. Transfer soup to blender; blend in batches to a puree. Pour puree back into saucepan. If soup is too thick, thin with more water or stock. Reheat. Ladle soup into bowls: garnish with parsley.

Cream Of Asparagus Soup

2 lbs. fresh asparagus
1 sm. onion, chopped
6 cloves roasted garlic
1 thin slice fresh ginger peeled and chopped
1 fresh green chili, seeded and chopped
2 med. boiled potatoes, peeled and cubed
½ c. fresh chopped parsley
8 c. vegetable stock, page 138
1 T. vegetable curry powder, page 198
1 tsp. dried Italian seasoning
Lemon pepper to taste
Yogurt for garnish

Wash asparagus; cut off tips and reserve. Peel stalks with carrot peeler; cut off woody ends; discard. Coarsely chop stalks. In nonstick saucepan, combine chopped asparagus stalks and rest of the ingredients except yogurt for garnish. On high heat, bring to a boil; reduce to medium heat. Cover and cook for 10 minutes or until tender. Let cool slightly; transfer soup to blender. Puree in batches. Return puree to saucepan. If soup is too thick, thin with more stock. Add reserved asparagus tips. Reheat soup for 5 minutes. Ladle soup into bowls. Garnish with a dollop of yogurt.

Minestrone

2 T. olive oil or canola oil
1 sm. onion, chopped
2 cloves garlic, chopped
2 med. tomatoes, chopped
2 T. tomato paste
1 tsp. vegetable curry powder, page 196
12 c. water
1 bay leaf
1 tsp. Italian seasoning
2 med. potatoes, peeled and diced
2 med. carrots, peeled and diced
1 stalk celery with leaves, chopped
Lemon pepper to taste
1½ c. fresh green beans (1-in. pieces)
1 med. zucchini, sliced
1 c. cooked kidney beans or canned beans, drained and rinsed
1 c. cooked elbow macaroni.

Heat a nonstick heavy saucepan on medium-high heat. Add oil; sauté onion, garlic, tomatoes and vegetable curry powder for 2 to 3 minutes. Add water, bay leaf, Italian seasoning, potatoes, carrots and celery. Add lemon pepper to taste. On high heat, bring to a boil; reduce to medium heat. Cover and cook until potatoes are tender; uncover. Add rest of the ingredients. Cover and simmer for 15 to 20 minutes, stirring occasionally. Serve hot.

Lentil Soup With Spinach

1 T. vegetable oil
1 sm. onion, chopped
2 cloves garlic, chopped
2 ripe tomatoes, diced
¼ c. fresh chopped parsley
1 tsp. cumin powder
1 c. red lentils, wash well until water runs clear
6 c. water
2 cubes vegetable bouillon, crushed
1 bunch fresh tender spinach, wash well to remove sand and trim tough stems
Salt to taste

Heat a large nonstick saucepan until warm, add oil and heat. On medium-high heat sauté onions, garlic, tomatoes, parsley and cumin for 2 minutes. Add lentils, water and crushed bouillon. On high heat, bring to boil; reduce to low heat. Cover and simmer until lentils are tender, stirring occasionally. Discard any foam that floats on top. Add spinach; cook until tender. Add salt to taste; remove from heat. Serve hot or cold.

Curried Squash Soup

2 ½ lbs. butternut squash, peeled, seeded and cut into chunks
8 c. water or stock
1 sm. onion chopped
8 cloves roasted garlic
1 stalk celery
1 bay leaf
1 tsp. Italian seasoning
1 tsp. vegetable curry powder, page 196
1 tsp. paprika
Lemon pepper to taste
Dash roasted curry powder, page 198

In nonstick saucepan, combine first 9 ingredients. On high heat, bring to a boil Reduce to medium heat; cover and cook until squash is tender. Let cool; discard bay leaf. Transfer soup to blender; blend to a smooth puree. Pour puree back into saucepan. If the soup is thick, thin with water or stock. Add lemon pepper to taste. Reheat 5 minutes, stirring constantly. Ladle soup into bowls; garnish with dash of roasted curry powder.

Spicy Red Onion Soup

2 T. olive oil
1 ½ lbs. red onions, halved and finely sliced
2 T. balsamic vinegar
6 c. vegetable stock or tamarind pepper broth. Page 138 or Page 120
1 T. instant chopped onion
1 T. ginger-flavored soy sauce
1 T. roasted curry powder, page 198
¼ tsp. cayenne pepper
Juice of half lime
Hot pepper sauce to taste

Heat nonstick saucepan on medium-high heat; add oil. Sauté onions for 2 to 3 minutes; add balsamic vinegar. Sauté onions until caramelized. Transfer 1 cup of caramelized onions into a bowl; set aside. Add rest of the ingredients except hot pepper sauce. On high heat, bring to a boil. Reduce to medium heat; cover and cook for 10 minutes. Uncover; add reserved 1 cup caramelized onions; stir. Add hot pepper sauce to taste; reheat 2 to 3 minutes. Ladle soup into bowls; serve with crusty bread.

Curried Tomato Soup

2 T. olive oil
1 sm. onions, halved and finely sliced
2 cloves garlic, chopped
1 thin slice fresh ginger, minced
4 med. tomatoes, halved, seeded and chopped
1 stalk celery, chopped
1 tsp. roasted curry powder, page 198
6 c. vegetable stock or water
1/3 c. tomato sauce
Lemon pepper to taste
1/3 c. fresh shredded basil for garnish

Heat a nonstick heavy saucepan. On medium-high heat, add oil. Sauté onion, garlic and ginger for 2 minutes, stirring constantly. Add tomatoes, celery and roasted curry powder; sauté 2 to 3 minutes. Add stock, tomato sauce and lemon pepper to taste. On high heat, bring to a boil. Reduce to medium heat; cover and simmer until tomatoes are tender. Remove from heat; ladle soup into bowls. Garnish with shredded basil.

Salads

Cucumber And Onion Salad

2 English cucumbers, washed, unpeeled and finely sliced
2 green chili peppers, seeded and chopped
1 sm. onion, finely sliced
Lime juice, salt and fresh ground black peppers to taste

In a bowl, combine cucumber, green chili peppers and onions. Toss. Add lime juice, salt and black pepper to taste. Mix well with hand. Serve with rice and curry

Watermelon Salad

½ seedless watermelon
Lemon pepper to taste
2 med. red onions, halved and finely sliced
2 fresh green chili peppers, seeded and finely chopped
Lemon pepper to taste

Slice thick slices from half of watermelon. Cut red part of watermelon into bite size pieces. Transfer to a bowl. Add lemon pepper to taste. Toss few times; chill until ready to serve. In a small bowl, combine onion and chili pepper; add lemon pepper to taste. Mix well with hand; chill until ready to serve. Before serving, drain water from chilled watermelon. Add the chilled onion and chili pepper. Toss over few times and serve.

Please see photo at back of book.

Eggplant Salad

2 med. eggplants, cut into 2 –in. pieces (grilled, broiled, baked or fried)
1 med. red onion, halved and finely sliced
2 fresh green chili peppers, seeded and finely chopped
1 T. country Dijon mustard
Lime juice and salt to taste
Dash sugar
Extra lime juice, if needed

In a bowl, combine eggplant and rest of the ingredients except lime juice. Gently mix with hand to combine. Add extra lime juice if needed; mix to combine. Serve with rice and curry.

Tomato, Onion And Basil Salad

1 lg. firm ripe tomato, sliced
Salt and fresh ground pepper to taste
1 med. red onion, halved and finely sliced
2 sm. fresh green chili peppers, seeded and finely chopped
Lime juice, salt and fresh ground pepper to taste
1 c. fresh torn basil leaves

Arrange sliced tomatoes on flat platter. Sprinkle salt and pepper; chill until ready to serve. Before serving, drain liquid from sliced chilled tomatoes. In a small bowl, add onion and chili pepper. Add lime juice, salt and pepper to taste. Mix well with hand to combine. Add fresh basil and toss. Spread on chilled tomatoes. Serve with rice and curry.

Parsley Salad

2 bunch fresh parsley
1 med. red onion, finely chopped
1 sm. green chili pepper, seeded and finely chopped (opt.)
Lime juice and salt to taste
Extra lime juice, if needed

Trim discolored leaves and tough stems. Rinse under cold running water to remove any sand. Transfer into a bowl of salted of water, wash well and drain water. Pat dry parsley with paper towels. Finely chop parsley; transfer to a bowl. Add onion and chili pepper. Add lime juice and salt to taste. Mix well with hand to combine. Add extra lime juice if needed. Serve with rice and curry.

Okra Salad

½ lb. sm. fresh tender okra (do not cut off tops)
1½ c. water
½ tsp. salt
1 med. red onion, halved and finely sliced
1 sm. green chili pepper, seeded and chopped finely
White vinegar, salt and fresh ground pepper to taste

Using wet paper towels, gently clean okra; set aside. Combine water and salt in saucepan. On high heat, bring to a boil; add okra. Reduce to medium heat; cover and cook okra until slightly ender. Do not overcook. Remove from heat; transfer to a bowl of iced cold water. Drain water; pat dry okra with paper towels; set aside. In a bowl, combine onion and chili pepper; add vinegar, salt and pepper to taste. Mix well with hand to combine. Add the okra; toss few times. Chill and serve with rice and curry.

Jicama Apple Salad With Almonds

1 med. jicama, peeled and diced
3 med. apples, cored and diced
2 T. lime juice
Dressing:
¼ c. champagne vinegar
2 T. creamy mustard
1 tsp. honey
1 T. olive oil
½ c. slivered almonds
2 T. fresh chopped parsley
2 c. baby spinach

In a glass bowl, combine jicama, apples and lime juice. Toss a few times. In a small bowl, whisk vinegar, mustard and honey; gradually whisk in oil. Pour over jicama and apples; add almonds and parsley; toss to coat. Chill. Arrange salad plates with baby spinach; top with salad and serve.

Passion Fruit Leaf Salad

4 c. tender passion fruit leaves
1 sm. red onion, chopped
1 sm. green chili pepper, seeded and chopped
Lime juice and salt to taste

Stem passion fruit leaves; place in a bowl of salted water. Drain water. Wash with fresh water and drain. Pat dry passion fruit leaves with paper towels or dry in a salad spinner. Finely shred leaves; transfer to a bowl. Add onion and green chili pepper. Add lime juice and salt to taste. Mix with hand. Add extra lime juice if needed. Serve with rice and curry.

Red Cabbage Salad

½ head red cabbage
1 red onion, halved and finely sliced
2 sm. green chili peppers, seeded and chopped
Lime juice, salt and pepper to taste

Cut cabbage in quarters. Slice core; discard. Place cabbage in a bowl of water with 1 teaspoon vinegar; let stand 5 minutes. Drain. Wash with fresh water and drain. Pat dry the cabbage with paper towel or dry in a salad spinner. Finely shred cabbage; transfer to a glass bowl. Add onion and green chili pepper; add lime juice, salt and pepper to taste. Mix well with hand. Add extra lime juice if needed. Serve with rice and curry.

Watermelon Salad With Yogurt

2 c. plain yogurt or soy yogurt
½ watermelon, seeded
1 sm. red onion, halved and finely sliced
1 fresh green chili, seeded and finely sliced diagonally
¼ c. fresh chopped chives
Lemon pepper to taste

Pour yogurt into a strainer; place strainer over a bowl for liquid to drain. Place in refrigerator until ready to make salad. Slice watermelon into thick slices. Cut red part into large bite-size pieces. Place in a salad bowl; chill. Drain any excess liquid. Add the strained yogurt to the watermelon and add rest of the ingredients. Using a wooden spoon mix well until combined. Serve over a bed of mixed greens.

Mango Salad

3 med. firm semi-ripe mangos
½ c. mango puree
Lemon pepper to taste
Baby spinach

   Peel mangoes and slice. Discard seeds. Cut mango into bite-size pieces. Transfer mango to salad bowl. Add mango puree and lemon pepper to taste. Chill. Arrange platter with baby spinach. Top with mango salad and serve.

Note:
To make mango puree, blend few pieces of mango with a little water or yogurt.

Classic Potato Salad

4 med. potatoes, boiled and diced
½ c. celery, finely sliced
½ c. fresh button mushrooms, sliced
½ c. black olives, sliced
1 red bell pepper, seeded and diced
1 green bell pepper, seeded and diced
¼ c. fresh chives, chopped
¼ c. sour cream
¼ c. soy mayonnaise
2 T. lime juice
½ tsp. hot sauce

   In a bowl, combine first 7 ingredients. Toss a few times and set aside. Whisk sour cream, mayonnaise, lime juice and hot sauce; add to salad. Toss a few times. Chill and serve.

Beet Root Salad

2 med. beets
¼ tsp. salt
¼ tsp. sugar
1 tsp. lime juice
1 med. red onion, sliced into rings
Lime juice and salt to taste
Romaine lettuce for garnish

Scrub and wash beets. Place beets in a saucepan, pour water to cover beets by 2 to 3 inches. On high heat, bring to a boil. Reduce to medium heat. Cover and cook until beets are tender. Add more water, if needed. Remove from heat and drain water. Under running cold water peel beets. Slice beets. In a bowl combine sliced beets, salt, sugar and lime juice. Mix with hand and chill. In another bowl combine onion rings, lime juice and salt to taste. Mix with hand. Chill. Before serving, garnish a salad bowl with lettuce. Arrange beets. Spread onion rings on top and serve. Serve with rice and curry.

Cucumber And Tomato Salad

1 med. English cucumber, finely sliced
1 c. cherry tomatoes, halved
1 green chili pepper, seeded and finely sliced
Lime juice, salt and fresh ground black pepper to taste
1 c. feta cheese, broken into sm. pieces

In a bowl combine cucumbers, tomatoes, and chili peppers. Toss and chill. Before serving, drain any water. Add lime juice, salt and black pepper to taste. Sprinkle feta cheese and toss a few times.

Mustard Green Salad

1 bunch mustard greens
1 med. red onion, chopped
Lime juice and salt to taste

Discard any discolored or spoiled leaves. Wash well, drain water and pat dry with paper towels. Finely shred mustard greens, transfer to a bowl. Add onions, lime juice and salt to taste. Mix well with hand. Use a little extra lime juice if needed. Serve with rice and curry.

Steamed Vegetable Salad

½ head cabbage, halved, cored and sliced
3 med. carrots, peeled and sliced crossways
½ lb. whole tender green beans, ends broken off and strings removed
2 med. yellow squash, cut into 1-in. pieces, lengthwise
Dressing:
¼ c. apple cider vinegar
1 T. garlic paste
1 T. country Dijon mustard
1 tsp. sugar
2 T. olive oil

Steam vegetables until tender; do not overcook. Transfer to bowl of ice water. Drain water; pat dry with paper towels. Transfer to salad bowl. Cover and chill. In a bowl, combine rest of the ingredients; whisk and chill. Before serving, pour chilled dressing over steamed, chilled vegetables. Toss a few times and serve.

Spicy Potato Salad

4 lg. boiled yellow potatoes (Yukon Gold)
1 celery stalk, finely sliced
1 sm. red onion, chopped
1 green chili, seeded and chopped
1 med. carrot, peeled and chopped
1 c. cooked kidney beans
½ c. chopped fresh chives
Dressing:
1/3 c. champagne salad dressing
1 tsp. prepared horseradish
1 T. spicy brown mustard

In salad bowl, combine potatoes, onions, green chili, carrots kidney beans and chives; set aside. In a small bowl, whisk ingredients for dressing; pour over combined ingredients. Mix well to coat. Chill and serve.

Cauliflower Salad

6 c. cauliflower florets
1 tsp. white vinegar
1 sm. red onion, chopped
2 sm. green chili peppers, seeded and chopped
Pinch celery seeds
Lime juice, salt and pepper to taste

Combine florets with vinegar in food processor; process until chopped. Transfer to a glass bowl; add onion, chili pepper and celery seed. Add lime juice, salt and pepper to taste; mix well with hand. Use extra lime juice if needed. Serve with rice and curry.

Note:
Chop cauliflower with knife, if no food processor, and
add vinegar and toss.

Spicy Pineapple Salad

1 sm. fresh ripe pineapple
1½ tsp. sweet and spicy mustard
1 tsp. paprika
½ tsp. cayenne pepper
1 tsp. sugar
¼ c. apple cider vinegar
Salt to taste

Discard crown of pineapple; cut off skin. Remove eyes with point of knife and discard; cut into quarters. Discard hard core. Cut pineapple into bite-size pieces; transfer to a glass salad bowl. Add rest of the ingredients; toss well to combine. Chill and serve.

Carrot And Zucchini Salad

1 c. shredded carrots
1 c. shredded zucchini
1 med. red onion, chopped
1 green chili pepper, seeded and chopped (opt.)
Lime juice, salt and fresh ground black pepper to taste

In a bowl, combine carrots, zucchini, onions and chili pepper. Toss a few times and chill. Before serving, drain any water. Add lime juice, salt and black pepper to taste. Mix well with hand. Serve with rice and curry.

Tropical Fruit Salad

1 sm. fresh sweet ripe pineapple
2 lg. ripe mangoes
2 sm. papayas
2 ripe passion fruits
2 T. date sugar (add more if desired)
1 tsp. rose water
1 tsp. vanilla

Discard crown of pineapple. Cut off skin. With point of knife, remove eyes from pineapple. Cut in half and then into quarters. Cut off core and discard. Cut pineapple into bite-size pieces; transfer to a glass or ceramic bowl. Peel mangoes, slice flesh and discard seeds. Cut mango slices into bite-size pieces; transfer to salad bowl. Cut passion fruit in half, holding over salad bowl to catch juices. Using a small spoon, scoop out seeds and pulp with juices into salad bowl. Add rest of the ingredients, toss a few times to combine, chill salad. Spoon into small salad bowls and serve, or top with ice cream and serve.

Fiesta Pasta Salad

½ c. soy yogurt
¼ c. Italian salad dressing
¼ c. creamy mustard blend
1/3 c. fresh parsley, chopped
1 (16-oz.) box trio Italiano pasta
½ lb. fresh tender asparagus, steamed slightly
1 med. carrot, peeled and julienned
1 c. cherry tomatoes
1 sm. red onion, halved and finely sliced
½ c. slivered almonds
Fresh ground black pepper to taste

In a bowl, whisk first 4 ingredients for dressing; set aside. Cook pasta according to package directions, transfer to a large glass salad bowl. Add rest of the ingredients; pour dressing and toss to combine. Chill and serve.

Green Bean Salad

2 c. water
½ tsp. salt
½ lb. fresh whole tender green string beans, snip off ends, remove strings
1 med. red onion, halved and finely sliced
1 T. lemon juice
2 T. honey mustard
Salt and fresh ground black pepper to taste

Into medium saucepan add water and ½ teaspoon salt. On high heat, bring to a boil. Add beans. Reduce to medium heat. Cover and cook until slightly tender. Remove from heat and drain water. Cool cooked beans in ice water. Drain and pat dry with paper towels. In a bowl combine beans and onion and set aside. In small bowl, whisk lemon juice and mustard, salt and black pepper. Pour over beans. Toss a few times. Chill and serve.

Avocado And Cherry Tomato Salad

2 lg. avocados, peeled
1 T. lime juice
1 c. cherry tomatoes
1 med. red onion, sliced
½ c. sunflower seeds
¼ c. fresh basil, chopped
Red leaf lettuce for garnish
Dressing:
3 T. white vinegar
3 T. olive oil
3 T. honey mustard

Cut avocados in half, lengthwise. Remove seeds. Cut into bite-size pieces. Add lime juice and set aside. In a salad bowl, combine cut avocados, tomatoes, onions, sunflower seeds and basil. Chill. Whisk vinegar, olive oil and mustard. Pour over salad and toss a few times. Arrange a platter with lettuce leaves. Spread salad on top and serve.

Potato Salad

4 med. Yukon Gold potatoes, boiled, peeled and cut into bite-size pieces
1 sm. onion, chopped
1 sm. fresh green chili, seeded and chopped
1 sm. red bell pepper, seeded and diced
1 stalk celery, finely sliced
1 med. carrot, peeled and chopped
2 T. prepared horseradish
¼ c. sweet and spicy mustard
¼ c. mashed silken tofu
¼ c. fresh lime juice
Salt and pepper to taste
Dash celery seeds

In a salad bowl, combine potatoes and rest of the ingredients. Using a wooden spoon, mix well to combine. Chill and serve.

Apple Salad With Almonds

4 med. apples, cored and cubed
1 T. lime juice
1/3 c. slivered almonds
¼ c. fresh parsley, chopped
2 T. fresh basil, chopped
2 T. soy mayonnaise
3 T. creamy mustard blend

Combine apples and lime juice in a glass bowl. Toss a few times. Add the rest of the ingredients and mix well to coat. Chill and serve.

Cottage Cheese And Grape Salad

2½ c. nonfat cottage cheese
2 c. green grapes, wash, pat dry with paper towels and cut into halves
2 T. sugarless lime Jello
2 T. fresh mint leaves, minced

In a salad bowl, combine cottage cheese and rest of the ingredients. Using a wooden spoon, mix well to combine. Chill and serve.

Green Leaf Trio

3 c. fresh tender baby spinach leaves
2 c. iceberg lettuce, torn up
2 c. romaine leaf lettuce, torn up
2 c. fresh watercress leaves
Dressing:
¼ c. Italian salad dressing
1/3 c. nonfat plain yogurt
2 T. fresh mint, chopped
Dash sugar

In a bowl, combine greens. Chill until ready to serve. In small bowl, whisk salad dressing, yogurt, mint and sugar. Chill. Before serving, pour dressing over greens. Toss well to coat.

Carrot Salad

3 med. carrots, finely shredded
1 med. onion, chopped
1 green chili pepper, seeded and chopped
Lime juice and salt taste
Dash fresh ground black pepper

In a bowl, combine carrots, onions and chili peppers. Add lime juice and salt to taste. Add dash of black pepper. Mix well with hand. Serve with rice and curry.

Please see photo at back of book.

Carrot And Onion Salad

1 c. shredded carrots or finely cut into matchstick strips
1 sm. onion, halved and finely sliced
¼ c. green onions, chopped
Lime juice, salt and fresh ground black pepper to taste.

Combine carrots, onions and green onions. Add lime juice, salt and black pepper to taste. Toss. Chill and serve.

Mixed Herb Salad

1/3 c. fresh parsley, finely chopped
1/3 c. fresh basil leaves, finely chopped
¼ c. fresh fennel leaves, finely chopped
¼ c. fresh dill weed, finely chopped
1 med. red onion, finely chopped
2 green chili peppers, seeded and finely chopped
Lime juice and salt to taste,
Extra lime, if needed

In a glass salad bowl, combine the first 6 ingredients and toss well. Chill until ready to serve. Before serving, add lime juice and salt. Mix well with hand. Can be served with rice and other curried dishes.

Chickpea Salad

2 c. dried chickpeas
1 med. onion, halved and finely sliced
1 red bell pepper, seeded and diced
1 green bell pepper, seeded and diced
2 T. olive oil
2 T. country Dijon mustard
1 T. lime juice
¼ T. garlic paste
1 tsp. dried basil
¼ c. celery seed
Garlic salt and fresh ground black pepper to taste

Wash dried chickpeas. Into a saucepan, add chickpeas. Pour water to cover chickpeas by 3 inches. Let soak overnight. Discard skins and peas that float to the top. Drain water. Pour fresh water to cover by 3 inches. On high heat, bring to a boil. Reduce to low heat. Cover and cook until tender. Remove from heat. Drain and set aside. In a salad bowl, combine chickpeas, onions and bell peppers. Whisk olive oil, mustard, lime juice and garlic paste. Pour over combined ingredients. Toss a few times. Add basil, celery seed and garlic salt and pepper to taste. Toss a few times. Chill and serve.

Pineapple And Mango Salad

1 sm. fresh semi-ripe pineapple
2 semi-ripe mangoes
3 T. red wine vinegar
1 T. Dijon rough mustard
1 T. paprika
1 tsp. sugar

Discard crown of pineapple. Cut off skin. With point of knife, remove eyes and discard. Cut pineapple in half and into quarters. Discard hard core. Cut pineapple into bite-size pieces. Transfer to glass salad bowl. Peel mangoes. Slice and cut into bite-size pieces. Transfer to salad bowl. Discard seeds or if preferred add to bowl. Add vinegar, mustard, paprika and sugar. With wooden spoon, toss and mix well. Chill and serve.

Dizzle Potato Salad

4 med. boiled potatoes, peeled and diced
1 celery stalk, finely sliced
1 sm. onion, chopped
1 med. carrot, peeled and chopped
1 c. canned kidney beans, drained and rinsed
½ tsp. poppy seeds
Dressing:
1/3 c. champagne salad dressing
1/3 c. lite sour cream
1 T. spicy brown mustard
1 tsp. sugar

In a salad bowl, combine potatoes, celery, onions, carrots, kidney beans and poppy seeds. Set aside. In a small bowl, whisk salad dressing sour cream, mustard and sugar. Pour over combined ingredients. Mix well. Chill and serve.

Snake Gourd Salad

1 sm. tender snake gourd (1 ½ to 2 lb.)
1 med. red onion, halved and finely sliced
2 sm. fresh green chili peppers, seeded and chopped
Lime juice and salt to taste
Extra lime juice to taste

Scrape off skinny surface of snake gourd. Slit in half; discard seeds with fibrous pulp. Rinse under running cold water. Pat dry with paper towels and slice finely. Set aside. Combine onion and green chili in salad bowl. Add sliced snake gourd. Add lime juice and salt to taste; mix well with hand. Add extra lime juice; toss few times to coat. Serve with rice and curry.

Bittermelon Salad (Called Bittergourd)

2 med. tender bittermelons
1 sm. red onion, halved and finely sliced
2 green chili, seeded and finely sliced diagonally
Lemon pepper to taste
Fresh lime juice to taste

Slice bittermelons in half lengthwise. Using a spoon, scrape out fibrous pulp with seeds; discard. Finely slice bittermelon diagonally; transfer to a bowl. Pour very hot water over melon to remove bitterness; drain water. Wash and rinse bittermelon a few times; squeeze out excess water. Transfer bittermelon to a glass bowl; add rest of the ingredients. Mix well with hands to combine. Serve with rice and curried dish.

Note: This vegetable is very good for diabetics
Note: Snake gourd and bittermelon are available at
Asian markets.

Rice Dishes

Biryani Rice With Shiitake Mushrooms

2 c. basmatic rice
2 T. olive oil or canola oil
1 sm. red onion, halved and finely sliced
2 sprigs coriander leaves
8 cherry tomatoes, halved
6 med. fresh shiitake mushrooms, cleaned with damp paper towels and woody stems removed
2 T. Biryani paste
1 T. vegetable curry powder, page 196
3½ c. vegetable stock
1 ½ c. coconut or soy milk
Salt to taste
½ c. chopped fresh coriander leaves

Place rice in a large bowl; cover with water 2 inches above rice. Set aside. Drain. Wash rice 3 or 4 times; drain water. Place rice in a colander to drain excess water. Heat nonstick heavy saucepan; add oil. On medium heat, sauté onions, coriander sprigs and tomatoes for 2 minutes. Add mushrooms, Biryani paste and vegetable curry powder; stir to coat mushrooms; sauté 2 minutes. Using tongs, transfer mushrooms to a bowl; set aside. Add rice to pan; sauté, stirring constantly, to coat grains. Add stock, milk and salt to taste. On high heat, bring to boil. Reduce to low heat; cover with a fitting lid. Cook 20 minutes; uncover. Add mushrooms; cover and let stand 12 minutes. Uncover. Using wooden spoon, toss rice and mushrooms and mix.

Mixed Rigatoni

1 (16-oz) pkg. rigatoni
2 T. olive oil or canola oil
1 sm. red onion, halved and finely sliced
1 med. tomato, chopped
1 med. carrot cut into matchstick strips (lengthwise)
1 c. sliced fresh mushrooms
1 med. zucchini, halved and sliced into 1-in. pieces
1 pkt. onion/mushroom mix, combined with 2 c. stock
1 (14-oz.) can artichokes, drained and rinsed
½ c. chopped fresh parsley
1/3 c. fresh grated Parmesan cheese
Lemon pepper to taste

Cook rigatoni according to package directions. While rigatoni is cooking, heat a nonstick heavy shallow skillet. Heat oil on medium-high heat and sauté onions, tomato, carrot, mushrooms and zucchini for 2 to 3 minutes. Add onion/mushroom mix combined with stock; add artichokes and parsley. Cook, stirring constantly until sauce is slightly thick. Add cooked rigatoni and Parmesan cheese; add lemon pepper to taste. Stir to mix well. Serve hot immediately.

Herbed Green Rice

2 med. sized green tomatoes, diced
4 green chilies, seeded and chopped
⅓ c. white vinegar
1 c. minced fresh coriander leaves
1 c. minced fresh parsley
Salt to taste
2 c. basmatic rice, washed 3 or 4 times, drained and set aside
3 ½ c. vegetable stock or water

Combine first 6 ingredients in a food processor or blender, blend to a smooth paste; set aside. In a nonstick heavy saucepan, combine rice, water and blended mixture. On high heat, bring to a boil. Reduce to low heat; cover with fitting lid. Cook 20 minutes. Do not lift lid. Let stand for 10 minutes. Uncover and fluff rice with fork to separate grains.

Basmati Rice, Soaking Method

2 c. basmatic rice
4 c. water
6 cardamom pods, bruised
1 ½ -in. stick cinnamon
1 bay leaf
4 whole cloves
½ tsp. olive oil or canola oil
Salt to taste

Place rice in a large bowl. Pour water to cover 2 inches above; set aside 20 minutes to release excess starch. Drain water. Wash rice 3 to 4 times. Place rice in a colander to drain any excess water. In a nonstick saucepan, bring 4 cups water to a boil. Reduce to medium heat. Add rice and rest of the ingredients. Bring to a boil on high heat. Reduce to low heat; cover pan with fitting lid. Cook 20 minutes; do not lift lid. Turn off heat; let stand for 10 minutes. Uncover and fluff rice with fork to separate grains.

Yellow Rice

1 med. square piece of cheesecloth
8 whole cloves
8 cardamom pods, bruised
10 to12 whole allspice
20 peppercorns
1 bay leaf
2 c. basmatic rice
3 T. vegetable olive oil or canola oil
1 sm. onion, halved and finely sliced
2 sprigs coriander leaves
½ tsp. turmeric powder
6 c. coconut milk or soymilk
Salt to taste
Carrots salad for garnish

In middle of cheesecloth, place first 5 ingredients. Hold cheesecloth together and twist to form a ball. Tie with cooking string so spices do not fall out; set aside. Wash rice 3 to 4 times; drain water. Place in a colander to drain excess water. Heat a nonstick heavy saucepan; add oil. On medium heat, sauté onions, coriander sprigs and turmeric; add rice. Sauté 2 minutes to coat rice; add tied spices, milk and salt to taste. On high heat, bring to a boil; reduce to low heat. Cover with fitting lid; cook 20 minutes. Turn off heat, uncover and discard tied spices. Fluff rice with fork to separate grains. Serve on to a platter; garnish around with carrot salad, page 163.

Please see photo at back of book.

Mixed Thin Rice Vermicelli

1(16-oz.) pkg. thin rice vermicelli
3 T. olive oil
1 sm. red onion, halved and finely sliced
1 thin slice fresh ginger, minced
1 med. tomato, chopped
1 clove garlic, minced
1 c. julienned carrots
1 c. julienned button mushrooms
1 c. julienned snow peas
1 c. julienned cabbage
¼ c. fresh parsley, chopped
Salt and pepper to taste

Break vermicelli in half. Place in a bowl; pour boiling water over vermicelli; cover and let stand 30 minutes. Drain water; cover and set aside. Heat a nonstick shallow skillet; add oil. On medium-high heat, sauté onion, ginger and tomato for 2 minutes. Add garlic, carrots, mushrooms, snow peas and cabbage, sauté for 2 to 3 minutes. Reduce to low heat; add vermicelli, parsley, salt and pepper to taste. Cook 5 minutes. Toss to mix. Serve on to a platter with curried dish of your choice.

Spinach Fusilli With Curried Red Kidney Beans

2 c. spinach fusilli macaroni
Dash olive oil or canola oil
1 T. olive oil or canola oil
1 sm. onion, halved and finely sliced
1 c. cherry tomatoes, halved
¼ c. fresh parsley, chopped
½ T. roasted curry powder, page 198
1 T. paprika
2 c. vegetable stock, page 138
2 c. cooked kidney beans or canned beans, drained and rinsed
Lemon pepper to taste

Bring large pan of water to boil, add fusilli and stir. Reduce to medium heat; cover and cook for 12 minutes or till slightly tender but still firm. Do not overcook. Remove from heat; drain water. Add oil and toss to avoid sticking. Heat nonstick shallow skillet; add oil. On medium heat, sauté onion, tomatoes, parsley, curry powder and paprika. Sauté 3 minutes; add cooked fusilli, stock and kidney beans. Stir. Add lemon pepper to taste; uncover and simmer until sauce is slightly thick. Remove from heat; serve hot.

Basmatic Rice

(No Oil Method)
2 c. basmatic rice
4 c. water
Salt to taste

Wash rice 3 to 4 times; drain water. In nonstick heavy saucepan, combine rice, water and salt. On high heat, bring to a boil. Reduce to low heat; cover pan with fitting lid. Cook 20 minutes; do not lift lid. Turn off heat; let stand for 10 minutes. Uncover; fluff rice with fork to separate grains.

Vegetable Lamprais Parcels

1 sm. square cheesecloth
8 cloves
1 ½ -in stick cinnamon
8 whole allspice
10 cardamom pods, bruised
2 c. basmati rice
3 ½ c. vegetable stock or water
Salt to taste
Square banana leaves for wrapping rice parcels, 12 x 16-inch
1 ¾ c. coconut milk
eggplant curry, page 94
Spicy curried cashew curry, page 41
Seeni sambol, page 194
Jackfruit cutlets, page 11
Cucumber and onion salad, page 148

Wash rice 3 to 4 times; place in colander to drain water.

In middle of cheesecloth, place first 4 ingredients; hold cheesecloth together and twist to form a ball. Tie with kitchen string; set aside.

In a nonstick saucepan, pour stock or water; add rice and tied spices; add salt to taste. On high heat bring to a boil; reduce to low heat. Cover with fitting lid; cook 20 minutes, do not lift lid. Turn off heat and let stand 10 minutes. Remove from heat; uncover and discard spices. Fluff rice with fork to separate grains.

Wash banana leaves carefully to avoid splitting. Hold each leaf above medium-low heat until the color of the banana leaf changes. Do not burn leaves. Place1banana leaf, 12 x16 inches on clean surface. Place 1 cup rice in middle of leaf; pour 2½ tablespoons coconut milk over rice. Spoon a small serving of eggplant curry, cashew nut curry, 1tablespoon seeni sambol and 1 Jackfruit cutlet around the side of rice. Carefully fold bananaleaf over to form a parcel; secure with toothpick.

Before serving, heat oven to 375 (F) degrees. Place parcels on baking tray;

reheat for 20 minutes. Remove from oven; transfer parcels to a flat platter and serve with side of cucumber and onion salad. When your guests open parcels, they smell the fragrance of banana leaf and aroma of food.

Note:
parcels should be made 4 to 5 hours ahead and
refrigerated; reheat as instructed

Note:
You can add Deviled Jackfruit with onions, tomatoes,
peppers and leeks, page 59.

Pasta In Curried Tofu Tamarind Sauce

2 c. cooked pasta of your choice
½ tsp. tamarind paste
¾ c. vegetable stock or water
1 sm. onion, chopped
2 cloves garlic, minced
1 thin slice fresh ginger, minced
1 pkg. silken tofu, mashed
1 tsp. paprika
1 ½ tsp. roasted curry powder, page 198
½ tsp. cayenne pepper
2 c. soymilk or coconut milk
¼ c. fresh chives, chopped
Salt to taste

In a small bowl, combine tamarind, stock or water; set aside. In a nonstick heavy shallow skillet, add tamarind mixture and rest of the ingredients except chives and salt to taste. On high heat, bring to a boil; reduce to medium heat. Simmer until sauce is thick, stirring occasionally. Add cooked pasta, chives and salt to taste. Simmer for 5 minutes; serve hot.

Racconto With Curried Lentil Sauce

3 c. racconto macaroni
Dash olive oil or canola oil
1 c. lentils
2 c. stock or water
1 sm. onion, halved and finely sliced
2 cloves garlic, minced
1 thin slice fresh ginger, minced
2 green chilies, seeded and minced
2 med. tomatoes, halved, seeded and chopped
1 T. vegetable curry powder, page 196
1 T. paprika
2 T. tomato paste
¼ c. tomato sauce
Lemon pepper to taste
¼ c. fresh chopped parsley

Bring a large pan of water to boil; add pasta and oil. Cover and cook 12 minutes or until slightly tender but still firm, stirring occasionally. Uncover; drain and rinse pasta under running cold water. Transfer to a bowl; set aside. In a large saucepan, combine lentils and rest of the ingredients except lemon pepper and parsley. Bring to a boil; reduce to medium heat. Cover and cook until lentils are slightly tender, stirring occasionally. Discard any foam that floats on top. Add lemon pepper and parsley; simmer 5 minutes. Add cooked racconto; stir. Simmer 5 minutes. Serve hot.

Curried Tomato Rice

2 c. basmati rice
4 oz. sun-dried tomatoes in oil, drained and chopped (reserve oil)
1 sm. red onion, halved and finely sliced
2 med. tomatoes, halved seeded and chopped
1 T. vegetable curry powder, page 196
3 ½ c. stock or water
½ c. tomato sauce
1 tsp. dried basil
Salt to taste
1 c. shredded fresh basil for garnish

Wash rice 3 to 4 times; drain water. Place rice in a colander; set aside to drain excess water. Heat a nonstick heavy saucepan; add reserved oil. On medium-high heat, sauté onion, tomatoes and vegetable curry powder for 2 minutes. Add rice; stir to coat grains and sauté 2 minutes. Add stock, tomato sauce and salt to taste. Add reserved chopped sun-dried tomatoes. On high heat, bring to a boil. Reduce to low heat; cover pan with fitting lid. Cook 20 minutes; do not lift lid. Turn off heat, let stand 10 minutes. Uncover; fluff rice with fork to separate grains. Spoon rice to platter; garnish with shredded basil. Serve with a curried dish and a salad of your choice.

Cinnamon Rice With Cashew Nuts, Raisins And Peas

2 c. basmatic rice
3 ½ c. vegetable stock or water, page 138
1 tsp. vegetable curry powder, Page 196
1 (2-in.) stick cinnamon
Salt to taste
1 T. olive oil or canola oil
1 sm. onion, halved and finely sliced
1 (1-in.) stick cinnamon
1 c. cashew nuts
½ c. raisins
½ c. frozen peas, thawed

Wash rice 3 to 4 times; drain water. Place rice in a colander to drain any excess water. In a heavy nonstick saucepan, combine rice, stock, vegetable curry powder and 2-inch stick cinnamon. Add salt to taste. Stir. On high heat, bring to a boil. Reduce to low heat; cover pan with fitting lid. Cook for 20 minutes. Do not lift lid. Turn off heat; let stand 10 minutes. Heat a small nonstick skillet; add oil. On medium heat, sauté onion and 1-inch stick cinnamon. Sauté 1 minute. Add cashew nuts, raisins and peas; sauté 2 minutes. Uncover rice; add sautéed ingredients. Using a wooden spoon, toss rice and mix well to combine. Serve with a curried dish and a salad of your choice.

Mixed Fried Brown Rice

2 c. brown rice
2 T. canola oil or olive oil
1 sm. onion, halved and finely sliced
1 c. fresh sliced mushrooms
1 ½ c shredded carrots
1 ½ c shredded cabbage
8 cherry tomatoes, halved
1 c. green onions, chopped
¼ c. lite-soy sauce
2 hard-boiled eggs, shelled and sliced
½ c. fresh parsley salad for garnish

Cook rice according to box directions, substituting stock instead of water. Cover and keep warm. Heat nonstick medium saucepan; add oil. On medium-high heat, sauté onion, mushrooms, carrots, cabbage, tomatoes and green onions for 3 to 4 minutes. Reduce to low heat. Add cooked rice and soy sauce; stir and mix well. Turn off heat; cover and let stand 10 minutes. Remove from heat. Fluff rice with fork to separate grains. Transfer to a platter; garnish with sliced boiled egg and parsley salad, page 151.

Milk Rice

2 c. basmati rice
5 c. water
Salt to taste
3 c. coconut milk or soymilk

Wash rice 2 to 3 times; drain water. In a nonstick heavy saucepan combine rice, water and salt. On high heat, bring to a boil. Reduce to low heat; cover and cook 15 minutes. Uncover. Add milk; cover and simmer 20 minutes or until milk is absorbed, stirring occasionally. Remove from heat. Immediately layer rice on a flat platter; let cool. Cut into squares Serve with seeni sambol, page 194.

Mixed Couscous

1 pkg. plain couscous
2 cubes vegetable bouillon
2 T. olive oil or canola oil
1 sm. red onion, chopped
2 green chilies, seeded and minced
1 med. carrot, peeled and chopped
1 c. cooked black beans or canned beans, drained
1 c. chopped green onions
1 c. dried cranberries
½ c. chopped parsley

Cook couscous according to package directions, adding vegetable bouillon cubes. Remove from heat; fluff couscous with fork to separate grains. Heat nonstick heavy shallow skillet; add oil. On medium heat, sauté rest of the ingredients except parsley. Sauté 5 minutes; add couscous and parsley. Stir to combine. Remove from heat. Fluff couscous with fork to separate grains. Transfer to platter. Serve with a salad of your choice.

Mixed Rice Sticks

1 pkg. rice sticks
2 T. olive oil
1 sm. red onion, halved and finely sliced
10 cherry tomatoes, halved
2 cloves garlic, minced
1 slice fresh ginger, minced
1 c. julienned carrots
1 c. julienned red peppers
1 c. sliced fresh mushrooms
¼ c. fresh parsley, chopped
Salt and pepper to taste.

Place rice sticks in a bowl; pour boiling water over; cover and let stand 15 to 20 minutes. Drain water; cut rice sticks in 4-inch lengths. Set aside. Heat nonstick heavy shallow skillet; add oil. On medium heat, sauté onion, tomatoes, garlic and ginger for 2 minutes. Add carrots, red peppers and mushrooms. Sauté 2 minutes; reduce to low heat. Add rice sticks, parsley, salt and pepper to taste; toss a few times. Remove from heat. Serve onto a platter with a curried dish of your choice.

Orzo Tofu Supreme

1 (16-oz.) pkg. orzo, cooked according to pkg. directions (transfer to a
bowl; add 1 tsp. olive oil to avoid sticking; set aside)
2 T. olive oil
1 sm. red onion, chopped
1 med. tomato, halved, seeded and chopped
1 c. sliced fresh button mushrooms
1 med. carrot, peeled and chopped
1 c. fresh celery leaves, chopped
1 pkg. firm tofu, cubed
1 ½ T. vegetable curry powder, page 196
Lemon pepper to taste
1 c. vegetable stock
½ c. fresh parsley, chopped

Heat nonstick heavy shallow skillet; add oil. On medium heat, sauté onion,
tomato, mushrooms, carrot and celery leaves 2 to 3 minutes. Add tofu, vegetable
curry powder and lemon pepper; toss. Sauté 2 minutes. Add stock; simmer for
5 minutes. Add cooked orzo and parsley; simmer 2 minutes and toss. Remove
from heat; transfer to a platter and serve hot or at room temperature.

Cooking Basmatic Rice Without Soaking

2 c. basmatic rice
3 ½ c. water
½ tsp. olive oil or canola oil
4 cardamom pods, bruised
4 whole cloves
1 bay leaf
Salt to taste

Wash rice well, 3 to 4 times; drain water. In a nonstick heavy saucepan, combine rice and rest of the ingredients on high heat. Bring to boil; reduce to low heat; cover pan with fitting lid. Cook for 20 minutes. Do not lift lid. Turn off heat; let stand for 10 minutes. Uncover; fluff rice with fork to separate grains.

This & That

Chickpea Dip

2 c. cooked chickpeas with ½ c. reserved cooking water
3 cloves garlic, minced
3 shallots. Minced
Juice of 2 lemons
3 tsp. tahini paste
4 T. olive oil
1 green chili, seeded and minced
¼ c. fresh coriander chopped

Combine chickpeas with reserved cooking water, garlic, shallots and lemon juice in blender. Blend well. Add tahini paste and 3 tablespoons olive oil; blend to a smooth paste, scraping down sides. Transfer into a bowl. Add green chili and reserved 1 tablespoon olive oil, mix. Garnish with chopped coriander. Chill and serve with Roti. Page 192.

Vegetable Filling For Pastry Pies

3 T. olive oil or canola oil
¼ c. onion, chopped
2 cloves garlic, chopped
Dash fresh peeled grated ginger
1 c. celery
1½ T. flour
1 ½ c. vegetable stock or water
1 med. carrot, peeled and diced
1 med. Yukon Gold potato, boiled, peeled and diced
1 c. button mushrooms, sliced
1 bay leaf
Vinegar, salt and pepper to taste
½ c. frozen green peas, thawed

Place a nonstick shallow skillet on medium-high heat add oil, and sauté onion, garlic, ginger and celery for 3 minutes. Add flour and stir. Quickly add stock or water, stirring constantly for 3 minutes. Add rest of the ingredients except green peas. Uncover and simmer until slightly thick. Remove from heat. Add green peas. Let stand to cool.

Note:
Cool completely before filling pastry shells.

Vegetable Filling For Egg Rolls

3 T. olive oil or soy oil
¼ c. onion, chopped
2 cloves garlic, chopped
Dash fresh peeled ginger, grated
1 med. carrot, peeled and chopped
1 ½ c. sliced leeks, green and white parts
1 c. button mushrooms, sliced
2 med. boiled Yukon Gold potatoes, mashed
½ tsp. vegetable curry powder, page 196
Lemon pepper to taste

Place a nonstick shallow skillet on medium-high heat. Add oil, heat and sauté onion, garlic ginger for 2 minutes. Add carrot, leeks and mushrooms, sauté for 3 minutes. Add mashed potato, vegetable, curry powder and lemon pepper to taste. Sauté 2 minutes, stirring constantly to combine. Remove from heat. Let cool.

Yogurt Coriander Dip

1 ½ c. plain yogurt or soy yogurt
1/3 c. fresh coriander leaves, coarsely chopped
2 fresh green chilies, seeded and minced
3 shallots, peeled and minced
Lemon pepper to taste

Line strainer with double cheesecloth; place over a bowl. Pour yogurt into strainer. Place a saucer over yogurt; refrigerate overnight to strain liquid. Discard liquid. Add rest of the ingredients to strained yogurt; mix well. Chill 3 to 4 hours for flavors to blend. Serve with pastries or rolls.

Avocado Dip

2 lg. avocados
Juice of 2 lemons
2 shallots, peeled and minced
2 cloves garlic, minced
3 T. yogurt
1 sm. tomato, seeded and chopped
2 green chilies, seeded and minced
2 T. chopped fresh coriander leaves

Cut avocados in half; remove pits. Scoop out flesh into a bowl. Add lemon juice and mix. Add shallots, garlic and yogurt to avocado and mix well. Add rest of the ingredients and toss; chill before serving. Serve with Roti, on page 192.

Spicy Black Bean Dip

2½ c. cooked black beans with 1 c. cooking liquid
½ c. plain yogurt
1 green chili, chopped with seeds
1 sm. onion, chopped
2 cloves garlic, chopped
1 thin slice fresh ginger, peeled and chopped
Juice of 2 lemons
¼ tsp. cayenne pepper
3 T. fresh coriander, coarsely minced
Dash of hot pepper sauce, (opt.)

Add cooked beans with ½ cup reserved liquid in food processor; add rest of the ingredients except minced coriander and hot pepper sauce. Process to puree, pulsing a few times, scraping down sides with rubber spatula. If puree is too thick, thin with remaining reserved liquid to desired consistency. Transfer to a bowl; add minced coriander and hot pepper sauce to taste. Mix well to combine. Cover and chill.

Note: This recipe can be made one day ahead.

Eggplant Yogurt Dip

2 med. eggplants
1 c. plain yogurt, strained overnight
1 sm. red onion, chopped
2 cloves garlic, minced
2 fresh green chilies, seeded and minced
1 med. tomato, halved, seeded and chopped
2 tsp. tahini paste (sesame seed paste)
Juice of 1½ lemons
2 T. olive oil
Dash hot pepper sauce

Prick eggplant all over with fork. Bake, grill or broil until charred and soft. Cool slightly; peel eggplant and coarsely chop. Transfer to bowl; add rest of the ingredients and mix well until incorporated. Chill and serve with Roti, bread or pita bread.

Roti

2 c. all-purpose flour
3 c. unsweetened shredded coconut
1 tsp. salt (add more if desired)
¼ c. finely chopped red onion or shallot
1 sm. fresh green chili pepper, seeded and chopped
1 c. cold water (add more if needed)
Flour for dusting and reserve additional flour if necessary

In a bowl, combine flour, coconut and salt. Add onion and chili pepper. Gradually add water and mix with hand to form a soft dough, but not sticky. Add more flour or water if needed.

Using ½ cup to measure dough, make a small ball. Repeat the same until dough is used up, set aside.

Dust surface and rolling pin with flour. Roll a ball of dough to a circle a little bigger than a saucer. Heat a nonstick skillet over medium heat. Place roti in a hot skillet and cook until golden brown patches appear; turn roti over and do the same. Transfer to a plate. Serve with coriander chutney, page 201 or spicy red coconut sambol, page 215

Note:
Make roti , wrap with wax paper and freeze. Thaw in refrigerator before using.

Serves 6 people.

Coconut Sambol

2 c. unsweetened shredded coconut
3 T. hot water
1 sm. red onion, chopped
1 sm. tomato, seeded and chopped
2 green chili peppers, seeded and chopped
2 T. paprika and dash of dry chili pepper flakes
Lime juice to taste
Salt and fresh ground pepper, to taste

In a bowl combine first 6 ingredients; add lime juice, salt and pepper to taste. Mix well with hand. Serve with Roti.

Seeni Sambol

2 lbs. red onions
3 T. tamarind liquid mixed with ¼ c. water
3 T. paprika
3 T. roasted curry powder, page 198
4 cloves garlic, minced
1 T. fresh ginger, peeled and minced
1/3 c. olive oil or vegetable oil
1 sm. onion, chopped
1 (1-in.) stick cinnamon
1 (1-in.) piece rampe, (screwpine), (Pandana), (opt.)
Few curry leaves or bay leaf, crushed
1 (1-in.) bulb lemongrass, bruised slightly
Salt to taste
3 T. sugar or more, if desired
Lime juice and salt to taste

Finely chop onions in food processor; transfer to a bowl. Add tamarind mixture, paprika, roasted curry, powder, garlic and ginger; stir to combine, set aside. Place wok or large nonstick shallow skillet over medium heat; add oil. Sauté onion, cinnamon, rampe, curry leaves and lemongrass for 2 minutes; add combined chopped onion. Stir. Add salt to taste; reduce to low heat, cover and simmer until onions are very soft and liquid is absorbed, stirring occasionally to avoid burning. The sambol should have an oily appearance. Add sugar, limejuice and salt to taste; uncover. Simmer for 10 minutes, stirring constantly. Remove from heat; let stand at room temperature for at leas 4 to 5 hours.

Note: Can be made days ahead and refrigerated. Reheat or serve cold.

Note: Peel onions, cut into quarters. Transfer to a bowl of ice water; let stand about 20 minutes. Drain ice water, pat dry with paper towels and chop in food processor.

Potato And Cashew Nut Filling

2 T. canola oil or olive oil
¼ c. onion, chopped
2 cloves garlic, minced
¼ c. fresh parsley, chopped
2 c. fresh cashew nuts, chopped
1 T. mild curry paste, page 196
2 med. boiled potatoes, peeled and mashed

Heat oil in a nonstick skillet on medium heat. Sauté onion, garlic, parsley and cashew nuts for 2 minutes. Add curry paste and mashed potato and stir to combine. Sauté 2 minutes. Remove from heat. Set aside for filling stuffed snake gourd, on page 52.

Easy Quick Method Of Roasting Garlic

2 whole lg. garlic heads
¼ tsp. olive oil

Place the garlic head on dry surface. Using your palm, press hard on the head of garlic to separate the cloves. Remove part of the papery skins. Leaving some of the skins on cloves, so the cloves of garlic, do not burn quickly. Heat a heavy-bottomed skillet over the burner on medium heat. Add garlic cloves and oil; toss. Cover and roast for 2 minutes. Uncover and roast garlic, stirring constantly, until slightly charred and soft. Remove from heat; let cool. Peel garlic; use it in cooking or freeze for use later.

Note:
Do not burn too much, as garlic will be bitter.

Mild Curry Paste

4 T. paprika
4 T. roasted curry powder, page 198
2 T. chopped fresh peeled ginger
2 T. chopped garlic
1/3 c. red wine vinegar
¼ c. tomato paste
1/3 c. canola oil or olive oil

Combine all the ingredients in a food processor or blender. Process to form a paste. Transfer into a container and refrigerate. Use as called in recipes.

Vegetable Curry Powder

¼ c. coriander seeds
1/3 c. cumin seeds
2 tsp. fennel seeds
3 tsp. fenugreek seeds
3 T. turmeric powder

Heat a nonstick heavy skillet until warm. Add coriander seeds, stirring constantly until slightly heated through. Transfer to a bowl. Repeat with cumin seeds, fennel seeds and fenugreek seeds. Remove from heat; transfer to a bowl. Add turmeric and mix to combine. Transfer to a coffee grinder; grind to a powder; let cool. Put into airtight container for use in recipes as needed.

Yellow Coconut Sambol

2 c. unsweetened shredded coconut
3 T. hot water
¼ tsp. turmeric powder
Lime juice, salt and pepper to taste
1 T. olive oil or canola oil
1/3 c. chopped onion
1 sm. tomato, chopped
Few curry leaves, (opt.)
1 sm. green chili pepper, seeded and chopped

In a bowl, combine first 4 ingredients. Mix well with hand; set aside. On medium heat, place a nonstick skillet; add oil and sauté onion, tomato, curry leaves and chili peppers for 2 minutes. Reduce to low heat. Add combined coconut mixture; stir constantly until heated through. Remove from heat; serve with Roti.

Roasted Curry Powder

¾ c. coriander seeds
½ c. cumin seeds
3 T. fennel seeds
¼ c. fenugreek seeds
1-in. stick cinnamon, broken into sm. pieces
1-in bulb lemongrass, finely sliced
Few cardamom pods, bruised
Few curry leaves or 1 bay leaf, crushed
1/3 c. paprika

Heat a nonstick heavy skillet until warm. Reduce to low heat and add coriander seeds. Heat until slightly brown, stirring constantly. Transfer to a bowl to cool. In the same skillet heat cumin seeds, fennel seeds and fenugreek seeds. Add the cinnamon, lemongrass, cardamom, cloves and curry leaves or bay leaf. Heat slightly, stirring constantly. Transfer to a bowl and set aside to cool completely. In a coffee or spice grinder, grind all ingredients to a powder. Transfer to a bowl add paprika and mix to combine. Transfer into an airtight container for use in recipes as needed.

Sri Lankan Omelet

2 T. canola or olive oil
1/3 c. chopped red onion
2 sm. fresh green chili peppers, seeded and chopped
1 sm. tomato, halved, seeded and chopped
1 c. sliced fresh button mushrooms
1 T. fresh chopped parsley
1 T. paprika
Lemon pepper or salt to taste
4 eggs
2 T. butter
2 T. fresh chopped parsley

Heat a small skillet over medium heat; add oil and sauté onion, chili pepper, tomato and mushrooms until just soft. Add parsley, paprika and lemon pepper to taste, set aside. Break eggs into a bowl. Add lemon pepper or salt to taste. Beat eggs with a fork until just mixed and foamy, set aside. Heat a 6 inch omelet pan or heavy skillet over low heat until just hot. Add 1 tablespoon butter; heat until sizzling, but not brown. Immediately rotate pan to coat bottom. Pour in half of the egg mixture. When egg begins to set, use a fork or spatula to draw uncooked egg mixture from sides to run underneath; repeat few times so egg rises slightly. Add half of the sautéed ingredients and fold omelet in half. Gently press omelet with spatula and cook for 1 minute. Turn omelet over and gently press with spatula and cook for 1 minute. Gently slide to a serving plate; garnish with 1 tablespoon chopped parsley. Repeat with remaining egg mixture and remaining ingredients to make more omelets.

Note:
Omelet should be fluffy but not dry.

Mint Chutney

3 c. fresh mint leaves
2 thin slices fresh peeled ginger
3 fresh green chili peppers, seeded and chopped
10 shallots
3 cloves garlic
¼ c. unsweetened shredded coconut
1 c. lime juice
Salt to taste

Combined all the ingredients, except salt to taste in a food processor. Process until blended. Add salt to taste. Process to blended. Transfer to a small bowl. Serve with Roti or egg rolls.

Note:
To retain color, freeze chutney in airtight container. For more spicy chutney, add chili peppers with seeds.

Coriander Chutney

3 bunches firm coriander leaves
6 fresh green chili peppers, seeded and chopped
2 thin slices fresh ginger
4 cloves garlic
6 shallots
½ c. white vinegar, more if needed
3 T. sugar (add more if desired)
1 T salt

Trim discolored leaves and tough stems. Rinse coriander leaves under running cold water to remove any sand. Transfer coriander leaves to a bowl of salted water. Wash well and drain water. Pat dry coriander leaves with paper towels. Transfer to food processor. Add rest of the ingredients; process until blended. Transfer to a bowl. Serve with Roti or egg rolls.

Note:
To retain color, freeze chutney in an airtight container.
For spicy chutney, include chili pepper seeds.

Love Cake

2 c. semolina
2 sticks butter at room temperature
Lemon rind of 2 lemons
2 c. sugar
6 egg yolks
3 c. chopped cashew nuts
1 ½ c. pumpkin preserve (opt.)
1 tsp. ground nutmeg
1 tsp. ground cinnamon
1 tsp. ground allspice
¼ c. rose water (rose extract)
3 T. almond extract
¼ c. cognac brandy
¼ c. Bees honey
1 egg white, beaten until foamy and stiff peaks form

Warm semolina on low heat until just heated through, stirring constantly. Do not burn or brown semolina. Remove from heat add butter and lemon rind. Using a wooden spoon, mix well to combine. Set aside 5 to 6 hours or overnight.

Brush deep square pan with melted butter. Line again with 2 sheets of waxed paper and brush with melted butter. Set aside. Preheat oven to 275(F) degrees

Using an electric mixer, cream sugar and egg yolks until light and creamy, with air bubbles forming. Add the semolina and butter mixture, beating well to combine. Add the cashew nuts, pumpkin preserve and spices. Beat to combine. Add the rose water, almond extract, brandy and bees honey; beat to combine. Gradually fold in the beaten egg white. Using a wooden spoon, mix well to combine. Pour batter into prepared pan and smooth evenly.

Bake on center rack of preheated oven for 1 hour; reduce temperature to 250(F) degrees. Cover cake with foil; bake for 1 ½ hours or until cake is golden brown and firm to touch, or insert skewer to center of cake; if skewer comes out clean, cake is done.

Remove from oven; set aside to cool completely. Invert cake on a baking sheet. Peel off wax paper from cake. Wrap with waxed paper again and store wrapped cake in airtight container.

Note:
Love cake tastes better and is moist if cake is made 2 to 3
weeks before Christmas.

Caramel Ginger Flan

2 c. sugar
1/3 c. water
1 T. lemon juice
2 cans evaporated milk
¼ c. sugar
2 T. fresh peeled grated ginger
8 lg. egg yolks
3 tsp. sugar
1 T. vanilla
2 T. dark rum or brandy, (opt.)

Combine water and sugar in a small heavy saucepan. Stir on low heat until sugar dissolves. Increase heat to high heat and boil until sugar turns golden brown. Add the lemon juice (do not stir). Occasionally brush down sides of pan with wet pastry brush and swirl pan around until syrup is dark amber in color.

Immediately pour hot caramel mixture into 6 custard cups or ramekin molds, dividing evenly. Immediately swirl around each custard cup to cover bottom and sides with caramelized sugar. Set aside to cool.

In a pan combine milk, sugar and ginger. On medium heat, boil milk mixture until just heated through, stirring constantly. Remove from heat; set aside to cool.

In a bowl, whisk egg yolks, sugar and vanilla extract. Gradually whisk in the milk mixture. Add the rum or brandy; stir. Strain the custard and pour custard over caramelized sugar in custard cups. Place custard cups in a roasting pan or ovenproof dish. Pour enough hot water into roasting pan to combine halfway up sides of custard cups. Cover tightly with foil or lids. Bake in preheated oven at 350(F) degrees for 45 minutes or until custard is slightly soft in center, but firm when touched.

Remove from oven. Remove custard cups from roasting pan; set aside. Remove foil or lids for custard to cool completely. Chill in refrigerator.

Before serving, run a small knife around edges of custard. Invert onto dessert plates. Pour caramel syrup around custard and serve.

Steamed Christmas Fruit Pudding

1/3 c. crystallized ginger or ginger preserves, chopped
1/3 c. cherries, chopped
1/3 c. currents
1/3 c. dates, chopped
¼ c. raisins
2 T. candied peel, coarsely chopped
¾ c. cognac brandy
1 ½ c. all-purpose flour sifted with ½ tsp. baking soda + ½ tsp. powdered cinnamon + ½ tsp. powdered nutmeg, set aside
6 oz. butter, room temperature
¾ c. light brown sugar
3 eggs
½ tsp. lemon rind
1 T. vanilla extract

In a bowl combine dry fruits with ½ cup brandy. Cover and set aside overnight.

Brush a pudding mold with lid brush inside lid with melted butter. Line base with double sheets of wax paper. Brush with melted butter.

With an electric mixer, beat butter and sugar in a bowl until light and creamy. Add eggs 1 at a time, beating thoroughly after each addition. Add the (sifted dry ingredients) alternating with dry fruit mixture and ending with the flour mixture. Add lemon rind and vanilla extract; mix to combine. Spoon pudding mixture into prepared mold and smooth evenly. Top with buttered wax paper.

Place the lid and cover lid with aluminum foil. Place a rack in a pot large enough to hold pudding mold, with space around. Set the pudding mold on top of rack. Carefully pour enough boiling water to pot to come halfway up sides of pudding mold. On high heat, bring water to a boil; reduce to low heat. Cover pot and simmer for 2 to 2 ½ hours, until pudding is done. Or insert skewer in center of pudding; if skewer comes out clean pudding is done.

Do not let pudding get too dry. Check for water level every ½ hour; pour more boiling water if necessary.

Remove from heat. Carefully remove foil and lid. Pour the reserved ¼ cup of brandy over pudding. Cover with lid; set aside to cool completely. Keep pudding at room temperature.

Before serving, remove pudding from mold. Peel off wax paper and invert pudding onto a platter. Serve with raspberry sauce, page 213.

Note:
Make pudding 2 days before Christmas.

Mango Custard

1 (1/4 oz) pkt. or 1 T. gelatin
3 T water
1 c. coconut milk + 1 c. water + 1/3 c. mango puree
1/3 c. sugar
1 tsp. pure vanilla extract or rose water
1 drop green food coloring

Sprinkle gelatin over water in a small bowl. Stir to soften and set a side. In a small pan combine coconut milk, water, mango puree, sugar and vanilla, heat on low-heat until it comes almost to a boil. Add the gelatin and stir to dissolve completely. Remove from heat and pour half of the mixture into blender. Pulse until mixture is cool and slightly frothy. Pour into molds, chill until just set. Keep the remaining half of mixture at room temperature. Add the green food coloring to the mixture and pour into blender. Pulse until mixture is cool and slightly frothy. Pour over already chilled custard and chill until completely set. To serve, dip molds in hot water, turn upside down to a plate.

Sauce:

½ c. mango puree + ½ c. passion fruit pulp w/ seeds

Combine both purees in a small bowl and stir. Pour around and on top of custard to garnish.

Please see photo at back of book.

Mini Pastry Vegetable Pies

4 c. all-purpose flour
1 tsp. baking powder
1 tsp. salt
2 ¼ sticks unsalted chilled butter, diced sm.
2 egg yolks, beaten and combined with ½ c. + 2 T. ice water and 1 T. vinegar
1 egg yolk, combined with 2 T. cold water for egg wash
Extra flour for dusting

To Make Pastry: Sift flour and salt in a bowl; add the butter, mix using fingertips, until mixture resembles a coarse meal. Gradually add egg yolks combined with water and vinegar. Toss with fork until dough is just moistened. Knead lightly on floured surface until dough holds together. Cover with plastic wrap and chill ½ hour. Meanwhile, make filling. Preheat oven to 425 (F) degrees. Roll out pastry. Cut out 10 rounds to fit 4-inch fluted loose bottom tart pans or muffin pans. Set aside. Cut out 10 more 4-inch rounds for pie lids. Fill in pastry cases with vegetable filling. Cover with pastry lids. Chill. Prick lids slightly with fork for steam to escape. Brush pies with egg wash. Cover edges of pies with strips of aluminum foil to prevent quick browning. Bake for 30 minutes. Reduce oven temperature to 375 (F) degrees. Remove foil and bake pies for 30 minutes or until golden brown and crispy. Remove from oven; set aside to cool. Transfer pies from pie pans to a plate; serve with salad of your choice.

Note:
Light handling is the secret of a flaky pastry. Do not open oven for first 30 minutes. Can substitute store bought frozen puff pastry.
Vegetable filling for pastry Pies on page 188

Note:
Once you place lids, chill in refrigerator for 20 minutes before baking.

Red Coconut Sauce

3 sm dried red chili peppers
½ c. boiling water
2 c. unsweetened shredded coconut
¼ c. lemon juice
4 cloves garlic
2 thin slices fresh peeled ginger
2 T. canola oil or olive oil
¼ c. chopped red onion
1 sm. tomato, chopped
Dash mustard seeds
Few curry leaves
2 c. coconut milk or soymilk
1 T. paprika
Salt to taste

Using rubber gloves, remove stems and seeds from dry chili peppers. Transfer dry chili peppers into a bowl. Pour boiling water over, cover and set aside for 20 minutes until dry chili peppers are soaked and soft. Add the dry chili peppers with liquid into food processor or blender. Add the coconut, lemon juice, garlic and ginger; process to a smooth paste. Heat a nonstick shallow skillet on medium heat. Add the oil; sauté onion and tomato for 2 minutes. Add mustard seeds and curry leaves; sauté until mustard seeds pops. Add the coconut mixture, milk, paprika and salt, stirring constantly until sauce is heated through. The coconut sauce should resemble the consistency of soup. Remove from heat.

Note:
Serve with Dosai Crepes, page 219

Vegetable Ribbon Sandwiches

1 pkg. cream cheese at room temperature
2 med. boiled beets, peeled and grated
Lime juice to taste
3 med. boiled carrots, peeled and grated
Lime juice to taste
1½ c. parsley salad, page 151
24 thin slices of white bread or rye bread

Divide cream cheese into 4 portions; set aside. Add the grated beets with 1 portion of cream cheese into a small bowl. Add lime juice to taste. Combine into a paste. Set aside.

Add the grated carrots with 1 portion of cream cheese into a small bowl. Add lime juice to taste; combine into a paste. Set aside.

Add the parsley salad with 1 portion of cream cheese into a small bowl; combine into a paste. Set aside.

Spread 1 side of each slice of bread with remaining portion of cream cheese. Place 6 slices of bread on clean surface, cream cheese side up. Spread beet root paste evenly. Top with 6 slices of bread, cream cheese side up. Spread carrot paste evenly; top with remaining 6 slices of bread, cream cheese side up. Spread parsley salad paste evenly; top with remaining 6 slices of bread, cream cheese side down. Press gently; trim crusts. Cut each sandwich into 3 strips.

Note:
Great for a party or afternoon tea.

Cucumber Sandwiches

1 med. English cucumber, thinly sliced
Lime juice, salt and fresh pepper to taste
½ c. butter, room temperature
¼ c. sweet and spicy mustard
24 thin slices of white bread or pumpernickel or rye bread
3 T. fresh dill, chopped

Arrange cucumber in layers on flat platter. Add lime juice, salt and pepper to taste. Chill in refrigerator until ready to make sandwiches.

Combine butter and mustard in a small bowl; combine to a paste. Set aside. Drain juices from cucumber, pat dry with paper towels; set aside.

Spread butter-mustard paste on one side each slice of bread. Place 12 slices on clean surface, butter-mustard side up. Arranged layers of slices cucumber; sprinkle with chopped dill. Cover with remaining 12 slices of bread, butter mustard side down. Press gently and trim crusts. Cut each sandwich into 4 triangles.

Note:
Great for afternoon tea.

Vegetable Sandwiches

½ c. cream cheese, room temperature
¼ c. sweet and spicy mustard
24 thin slices of white bread or wheat bread
2 med. boiled beets, peeled and thinly sliced
3 med. boiled carrots, peeled and thinly sliced diagonally
2 c. fresh baby spinach

Combine cream cheese and mustard in a small bowl. Spread cream cheese and mustard on one side of each slice of the bread. Place 6 slices of bread on clean surface, cream cheese and mustard side up. Arrange layers of sliced beets. Top with 6 slices of bread, cream cheese and mustard side up. Arranged layers of sliced carrot. Top with 6 more slices of bread, cream cheese and mustard side up. Arranged layers of spinach. Top with remaining 6 slices of bread, cream cheese and mustard side down. Press gently and trim crusts. Cut each sandwich into 4 triangles.

Note:
Great for lunch or a light dinner with a cup of soup

Raspberry Sauce

2 pt. raspberries
¼ c. confectioners' sugar
1 tsp. lemon juice
1/3 c. soy yogurt or buttermilk

Rinse raspberry under cold running water; gently pat dry with paper towels. Transfer to a blender. Add sugar, lemon juice and yogurt; blend to a puree. Strain through a sieve into a bowl; chill in refrigerator until ready to serve.

Note:
Sauce should be made the same day as needed. Serve
with steamed Christmas fruit pudding page 206.

Tropical Salsa

2 c. chopped semi-ripe mango
2 c. chopped fresh pineapple
2 c. chopped semi-ripe papaya
1 sm. red onion, finely chopped
2 sm. fresh green chili peppers, seeded and chopped
2 T. fresh cilantro leaves chopped
Lemon pepper to taste

Combine first 5 ingredients in a bowl. Add the cilantro and lemon pepper to taste; toss few times. Cover and refrigerate until ready to serve.

Pickled Vegetables

1 1/3 c. apple cider vinegar
½ c. water
1 /3 c. Dijon mustard
2 T. sugar
1 T. salt
2 med. carrots, peeled and sliced diagonally
½ lb. whole tender string beans trim ends and remove strings
6 banana peppers, halved and seeded
20 shallots, peeled
3 whole dill pickles, quartered
½ lb. dates stoned and halved

Combine first 5 ingredients into a stainless steel saucepan. On high heat, bring to a boil; reduce to medium heat. Add the carrots, beans and banana peppers. Cook for 1 minute. Remove saucepan from heat. Cover and set aside for 10 minutes. Uncover; add rest of the ingredients. Using a wooden spoon, toss pickled vegetables well to coat with sauce. Transfer to a plastic container and refrigerate. Serve with rice and curry.

Note: Stir and mix vegetables to coat with sauce at least once a day.

Cranberry Raisin Chutney

4 c. fresh cranberries, rinsed
2 c. raisins
¼ c. fresh peeled grated ginger
½ c. red wine vinegar
1/3 c. sugar, (opt.)
¼ c. paprika
Salt to taste.

Combine all the ingredients in a nonstick saucepan. Cover and cook on medium heat until cranberries pop over. Uncover; reduce to low heat. Simmer to a thick consistency. Remove from heat; set aside to cool. Transfer into small plastic containers and refrigerate. Use with appetizers, Roti or to accompany rice and curry.

Note:
Chutney can be frozen, thaw at room temperature before
serving.

Spicy Red Coconut Sambol

2 c. unsweetened shredded coconut
¼ c. hot water
1 T. cayenne pepper
½ tsp. dry chili pepper flakes
6 shallots, peeled and finely sliced
1 sm. fresh green chili pepper, seeded and chopped
Lime juice, salt and pepper to taste

Blend or process first 4 ingredients; transfer into a bowl. Add the shallots and chili peppers; add lime juice, salt and pepper to taste. Mix well with hand. Serve with roti or serve with rice and curry.

Artichoke Spinach Dip

1 (13-oz.) can artichoke hearts, drained and coarsely chopped
2 (10-oz.) pkgs. Frozen spinach, thawed and squeezed well to dry
1 fresh green chili, seeded and minced
2 cloves garlic, minced
4 shallots, peeled and minced
½ c. sour cream
1/3 c. grated fresh Parmesan cheese
Lime juice to taste
Hot pepper sauce to taste

Combine all ingredients in a bowl; mix well to combine. Spray baking dish with olive oil spray. Spoon mixture into dish and spread evenly. Cover with aluminum foil; bake in preheated oven (375) (F) degrees for 10 minutes. Uncover; stir. Bake 10 minutes more; remove from oven. Serve with Roti **page 192** or crackers.

Tropical Fruit Chutney

4 c. pineapple, diced
3 c. ripe mango, diced
2 c. chopped dates
¼ c. fresh peeled grated ginger
¼ c. paprika
¾ c. red wine vinegar
Salt to taste
Sugar to taste, if desired

Combine all the ingredients in nonstick saucepan, except sugar to taste. Cover and cook on medium heat until fruits are tender; uncover. Reduce to low heat; simmer to a thick consistency, stirring constantly. Remove from heat; set aside to cool. Transfer into small plastic containers and refrigerate. Use with appetizers, roti or to accompany rice and curry.

Note: Chutney can be frozen. Thaw at room temperature before serving.
Note: If using sugar, add with combined ingredients and cook.

How To Boil Jackfruit

1 sm. tender jackfruit
Water to cover
Dash turmeric
Few pieces goraka (gamboge)
Salt to taste

Cut tender Jackfruit into small pieces. Place in a large saucepan. Pour water to cover Jackfruit 4 to 5 inches above. Add rest of the ingredient; bring to boil on high heat. Reduce to medium heat. Cover and simmer until Jackfruit is tender, stirring occasionally. Add more water, if needed. Remove from heat; set aside to cool. Drain water; discard goraka. Cut off skin from Jackfruit; cut off the center. Discard the skin and center. Cut boiled Jackfruit into slices and use as called for in recipes.

Note:
Boil jackfruit with skin.

Dosai Crepes

1½ c. split urad dhal flour
1 tsp. baking powder
2 c. rice flour
1 c. all-purpose flour
4 c. water
2½ c. coconut milk or soymilk
Salt to taste
Vegetable cooking spray

In a bowl, combine first 4 ingredients. Gradually add the water; whisk or blend to a smooth batter to the consistency of a thick cream to coat spoon. Cover and set aside at room temperature 5 to 6 hours or overnight. Before making crepes, gradually whisk in the milk; add salt to taste. Batter should be the consistency of a pancake batter. If batter is too thick, thin batter by adding more milk. Stir to combine, set aside. Heat 12-inch skillet on medium heat. Lightly spray with cooking spray. Using a paper towel, wipe skillet. Ladle ¼ cup batter; lift skillet immediately and rotate in a circular motion to form a pancake. Immediately return skillet to medium heat. Cook dosai crepe until slightly golden brown. Using a spatula, turn doasi crepe over and cook slightly until golden brown. Transfer dosai crepe to a flat platter. Repeat until all batter is used. Serve with red coconut sauce, page 210.

Note:
Split urad dhal flour can be purchased from an Indian grocery.

Jackfruit Cutlets
Recipe Page 11

please replace with colour insesrts

Sri Lankan Egg Rolls
Recipe Page 13

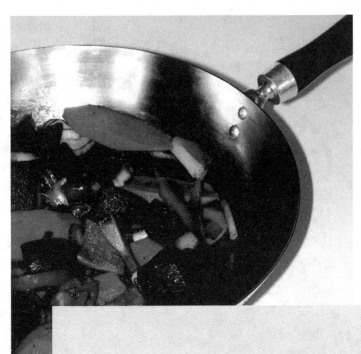

Deviled Beets and Carrots
Recipe Page 82

please replace with colour insesrts

Spicy Stir-fry Okra Sauteed with Onions and Dry Chili Flakes
Recipe Page 90

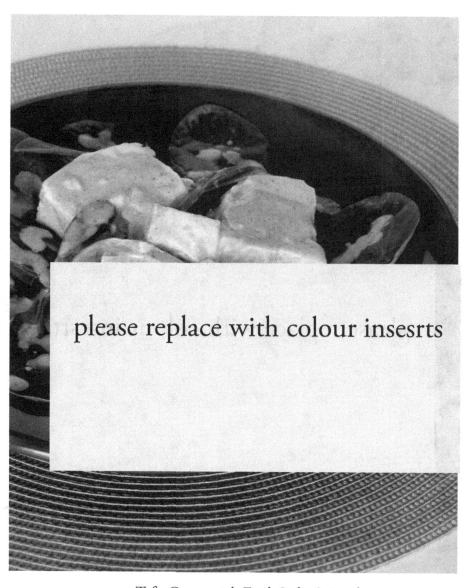

Tofu Curry with Fresh Baby Spinach
Recipe Page 101

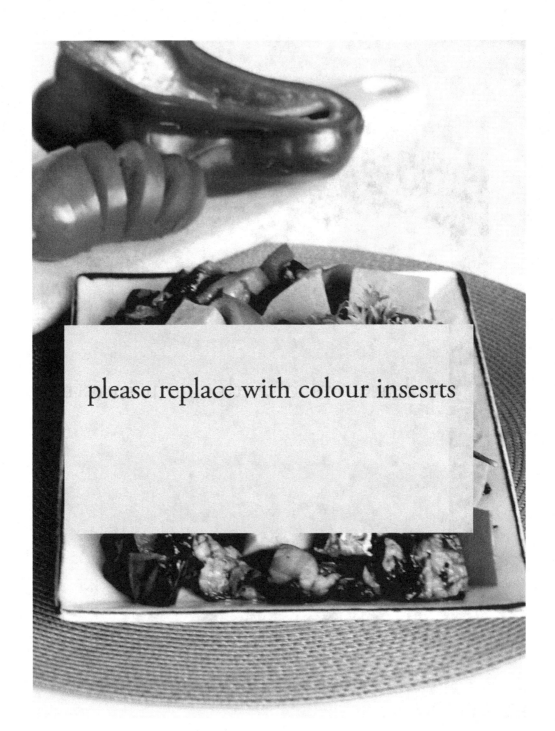

please replace with colour insesrts

Sweet Potato with Eggplant
Recipe Page 114

Watermelon Salad
Recipe Page 149

please replace with colour insesrts

Carrot Salad
Recipe Page 163

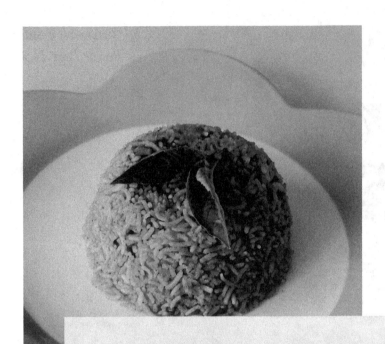

Yellow Rice
Recipe Page 172

please replace with colour insesrts

Mango Custard
Recipe Page 208

Index of Recipes

COOKING TIPS

- After stewing a chicken for diced meat for casseroles, etc., let cool in broth before cutting into chunks–it will have twice the flavor.

- To slice meat into thin strips, as for Chinese dishes–partially freeze and it will slice easily.

- A roast with the bone in will cook faster than a boneless roast–the bone carries the heat to the inside of the roast quicker.

- Never cook a roast cold–let stand for a least an hour at room temperature. Brush with oil before and during roasting–the oil will seal in the juices.

- For a juicier hamburger add cold water to the beef before grilling (1/2 cup to 1 pound of meat).

- To freeze meatballs, place them on a cookie sheet until frozen. Place in plastic bags and they will stay separated so that you may remove as many as you want.

- To keep cauliflower white while cooking–add a little milk to the water.

- When boiling corn, add sugar to the water instead of salt. Salt will toughen the corn.

- To ripen tomatoes–put them in a brown paper bag in a dark pantry and they will ripen overnight.

- Do not use soda to keep vegetables green. It destroys Vitamin C.

- When cooking cabbage, place a small tin cup or can half full of vinegar on the stove near the cabbage. It will absorb all odor from it.

- Potatoes soaked in salt water for 20 minutes before baking will bake more rapidly.

- Let raw potatoes stand in cold water for at least half an hour before frying to improve the crispness of French fried potatoes.

- Use greased muffin tins as molds when baking stuffed green peppers.

- A few drops of lemon juice in the water will whiten boiled potatoes.

- Buy mushrooms before they "open." When stems and caps are attached snugly, mushrooms are truly fresh.

- Do not use metal bowls when mixing salads. Use wooden, glass or china.

- Lettuce keeps better if you store in refrigerator without washing first so that the leaves are dry. Wash the day you are going to use.

- To keep celery crisp–stand it up in a pitcher of cold, salted water and refrigerate.

- Don't despair if you've oversalted the gravy. Stir in some instant mashed potatoes and you'll repair the damage. Just add a little more liquid to offset the thickening.

MEASUREMENTS & SUBSTITUTIONS

Measurements

a pinch	1/8 teaspoon or less
3 teaspoons	1 tablespoon
4 tablespoons	1/4 cup
8 tablespoons	1/2 cup
12 tablespoons	3/4 cup
16 tablespoons	1 cup
2 cups	1 pint
4 cups	1 quart
4 quarts	1 gallon
8 quarts	1 peck
4 pecks	1 bushel
16 ounces	1 pound
32 ounces	1 quart
8 ounces liquid	1 cup
1 ounce liquid	2 tablespoons

(For liquid and dry measurements use standard measuring spoons and cups. All measurements are level.)

Substitutions

Ingredient	Quantity	Substitute
self rising flour	1 cup	1 cup all-purpose flour, 1/2 tsp. salt, and 1 tsp. baking powder
cornstarch	1 tablespoon	2 T. flour or 2 tsp. quick-cooking tapioca
baking powder	1 teaspoon	1/4 tsp. baking soda plus 1/2 tsp. cream of tartar
powdered sugar	1 cup	1 c. granulated sugar plus 1 tsp. cornstarch
brown sugar	1/2 cup	2 T. molasses in 1/2 c. granulated sugar
sour milk	1 cup	1 T. lemon juice or vinegar plus sweet milk to make 1 c. (let stand 5 minutes).
whole milk	1 cup	1/2 c. evaporated milk plus 1/2 c. water
cracker crumbs	3/4 cup	1 c. bread crumbs
chocolate	1 square (1 oz.)	3 or 4 T. cocoa plus 1 T. butter*
fresh herbs	1 tablespoon	1 tsp. dried herbs
fresh onion	1 small	1 T. instant minced onion, rehydrated
dry mustard	1 teaspoon	1 T. prepared mustard
tomato juice	1 cup	1/2 c. tomato sauce plus 1/2 c. water
catsup or chili sauce	1 cup	1 c. tomato sauce plus 1/2 c. sugar and 2 T. vinegar (for use in cooking).
dates	1 lb.	1 1/2 c. dates, pitted and cut
bananas	3 medium	1 c. mashed
min. marshmallows	10	1 lg. marshmallow

*In substituting cocoa for chocolate in cakes, the amount of flour must be reduced.
Brown and White Sugars: Usually may be used interchangeably.

MICROWAVE HINTS

1. Place an open box of hardened brown sugar in the microwave oven with 1 cup hot water. Microwave at high for 1 1/2 to 2 minutes for 1/2 pound or 2 to 3 minutes for 1 pound.

2. Soften hard ice cream by microwaving at 30% power. One pint will take 15 to 30 seconds; one quart, 30-45 seconds; and one-half gallon 45-60 seconds.

3. One stick of butter or margarine will soften in 1 minute when microwaved at 20% power.

4. Soften one 8-ounce package of cream cheese by microwaving at 30% power for 2 to 2 1/2 minutes. One 3-ounce package of cream cheese will soften in 1 1/2 to 2 minutes.

5. Thaw frozen orange juice right in the container. Remove the top metal lid. Place the opened container in the microwave and heat on high power 30 seconds for 6 ounces and 45 seconds for 12 ounces.

6. Thaw whipped topping...a 4 1/2 ounce carton will thaw in 1 minute on the defrost setting. Whipped topping should be slightly firm in the center but it will blend well when stirred. Do not overthaw!

7. Soften Jello that has set up too hard—perhaps you were to chill it until slightly thickened and forgot it. Heat on a low power setting for a very short time.

8. Heat hot packs in a microwave oven. A wet finger tip towel will take about 25 seconds. It depends on the temperature of the water used to wet the towel.

9. To scald milk, cook 1 cup for 2 to 2 1/2 minutes, stirring once each minute.

10. To make dry bread crumbs, cut 6 slices bread into 1/2-inch cubes. Microwave in 3-quart casserole 6-7 minutes, or until dry, stirring after 3 minutes. Crush in blender.

11. Refresh stale potato chips, crackers or other snacks of such type by putting a plateful in the microwave oven for about 30-45 seconds. Let stand for 1 minute to crisp. Cereals can also be crisped.

12. Nuts will be easier to shell if you place 2 cups of nuts in a 1-quart casserole with 1 cup of water. Cook for 4 to 5 minutes and the nutmeats will slip out whole after cracking the shell.

13. For stamp collectors: place a few drops of water on stamp to be removed from envelope. Heat in the microwave for 20 seconds and the stamp will come right off.

14. Using a round dish instead of a square one eliminates overcooked corners in baking cakes.

15. A crusty coating of chopped walnuts surrounding many microwave cooked cakes and quick breads enhances the looks and eating quality. Sprinkle a layer of medium, finely chopped walnuts evenly onto the bottom and side of a ring pan or bundt cake pan. Pour in batter and microwave as recipe directs.

16. Do not salt foods on the surface as it causes dehydration and toughens the food. Salt after you remove from the oven unless the recipe calls for using salt in the mixture.

17. Heat left-over custard and use it as frosting for a cake.

18. Melt marshmallow cream in the microwave oven. Half of a 7-ounce jar will melt in 35-40 seconds on high. Stir to blend.

19. Toast coconut in the microwave. Watch closely as it browns quickly once it begins to brown. Spread 1/2 cup coconut in a pie plate and cook for 3-4 minutes, stirring every 30 seconds after 2 minutes.

Herbs & Spices

Get acquainted with herbs and spices. Add in small amounts, 1/4 teaspoon for each 4 servings. Taste before adding more. Crush dried herbs or snip fresh herbs before using. If substituting fresh for dried, use 3 times more fresh herbs.

Basil
Sweet warm flavor with an aromatic odor, used whole or ground. Good with lamb, fish, roast, stews, ground beef, vegetables, dressing and omelets.

Bay Leaves
A pungent flavor, use whole leaf but remove before serving. Good in vegetable dishes, fish and seafood, stews and pickles.

Caraway
Has a spicy smell and aromatic taste. Use in cakes, breads, soups, cheese and sauerkraut.

Chives
Sweet mild flavor of onion, this herb is excellent in salads, fish, soups and potatoes.

Curry Powder
A number of spices combined to proper proportions to give a distinct flavor to such dishes as meat, poultry, fish and vegetables.

Dill
Both seeds and leaves of dill are flavorful. Leaves may be used to garnish or cook with fish, soup, dressings, potatoes and beans. Leaves or the whole plant may be used to spice dill pickles.

Fennel
Both seeds and leaves are used. It has a sweet hot flavor. Use in small quantities in pies and baked goods. Leaves can be boiled with fish.

Ginger
A pungent root, this aromatic spice is sold fresh, dried, or ground. Used in pickles, preserves, cakes, cookies, soups and meat dishes.

Herbs & Spices

Marjoram   May be used both dry or green. Used to flavor fish, poultry, omelets, lamb, stew, stuffing and tomato juice.

Mint   Leaves are aromatic with a cool flavor. Excellent in beverages, fish, cheese, lamb, soup, peas, carrots, and fruit desserts.

Oregano   Strong aromatic odor, use whole or ground to spice tomato juice, fish, eggs, pizza, omelets, chili, stew, gravy, poultry and vegetables.

Paprika   A bright red pepper, this spice is used in meat, vegetables and soups. Can be used as a garnish for potatoes, salads or eggs.

Parsley   Best when used fresh but can be used dry. Use as garnish or seasoning. Try in fish, omelets, soup, meat, stuffing and mixed greens.

Rosemary   Very aromatic, used fresh or dried. Season fish, stuffing, beef, lamb, poultry, onions, eggs and bread.

Saffron   Orange yellow in color, this spice is used to flavor or color foods. Use in soup, chicken, rice and fancy breads.

Sage   Use fresh or dried. The flowers are sometimes used in salads. May be used in tomato juice, fish, fondue, omelets, beef, poultry, stuffing, cheese spreads, cornbread and biscuits.

Tarragon   Leaves have a pungent, hot taste. Use to flavor sauces, salads, meat, poultry, tomatoes and dressings.

NAPKIN FOLDING

General Tips:
Use linen napkins if possible, well starched.
For the more complicated folds, 24 inch napkins work best.
Practice the folds with newspapers.
Children can help. Once they learn the folds, they will have fun!

Shield

This fold is easy. Elegant with Monogram in Corner.

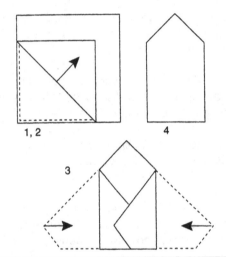

Instructions:
1. Fold into quarter size. If monogrammed, ornate corner should face down.
2. Turn up folded corner three-quarters.
3. Overlap right and left side points.
4. Turn over; adjust sides so that they are even, single point in center.
5. Place point up or down on plate, or left of plate.

Rosette

Elegant on Plate.

Instructions:
1. Fold top and bottom edges to the center, leaving 1/2" opening along the center.
2. Pleat firmly from the left edge. Sharpen edges with hot iron.
3. Pinch center together. If necessary, use small piece of pipe cleaner to secure and top with single flower.
4. Spread out rosette.

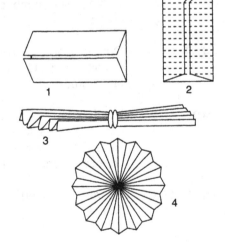

NAPKIN FOLDING

Fan

Pretty in Napkin Ring, or Top of Plate.

Instructions:
1. Fold top and bottom edges to the center.
2. Fold top and bottom edges to center a second time.
3. Pleat firmly from the left edge. Sharpen edges with a hot iron.
4. Spread out fan. Balance flat folds on each side on table. Well-starched napkins will hold the shape.

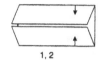

1, 2

4

3

Candle

Easy to do; can be decorated.

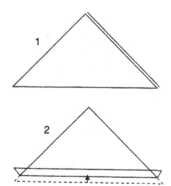

1

2

Instructions:
1. Fold into triangle, point at top.
2. Turn lower edge up 1".
3. Turn over, folded edge down.
4. Roll tightly from left to right.
5. Tuck in corner. Stand upright.

Lily

Effective and Pretty on Table.

Instructions:
1. Fold napkin into quarters.
2. Fold into triangle, closed corner to open points.
3. Turn two points over to other side. (Two points are on either side of closed point.) Pleat.
4. Place closed end in glass. Pull down two points on each side and shape.

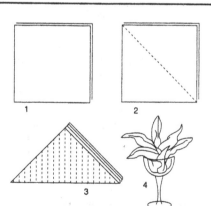

1

2

3

4

VEGETABLE TIME TABLE

Vegetable	Cooking Method	Time
Asparagus Tips	Boiled....................	10-15 minutes
Artichokes, French	Boiled....................	40 minutes
	Steamed................	45-60 minutes
Beans, Lima	Boiled....................	20-40 minutes
	Steamed................	60 minutes
Beans, String	Boiled....................	15-35 minutes
	Steamed................	60 minutes
Beets, young with skin	Boiled....................	30 minutes
	Steamed................	60 minutes
	Baked....................	70-90 minutes
Beets, old	Boiled or Steamed...	1-2 hours
Broccoli, flowerets	Boiled....................	5-10 minutes
Broccoli, stems	Boiled....................	20-30 minutes
Brussel Sprouts	Boiled....................	20-30 minutes
Cabbage, chopped	Boiled....................	10-20 minutes
	Steamed................	25 minutes
Cauliflower, stem down	Boiled....................	20-30 minutes
Cauliflower, flowerets	Boiled....................	8-10 minutes
Carrots, cut across	Boiled....................	8-10 minutes
	Steamed................	40 minutes
Corn, green, tender	Boiled....................	5-10 minutes
	Steamed................	15 minutes
	Baked....................	20 minutes
Corn on the cob	Boiled....................	8-10 minutes
	Steamed................	15 minutes
Eggplant, whole	Boiled....................	30 minutes
	Steamed................	40 minutes
	Baked....................	45 minutes
Parsnips	Boiled....................	25-40 minutes
	Steamed................	60 minutes
	Baked....................	60-75 minutes
Peas, green	Boiled or Steamed...	5-15 minutes
Potatoes	Boiled....................	20-40 minutes
	Steamed................	60 minutes
	Baked....................	45-60 minutes
Pumpkin or Squash	Boiled....................	20-40 minutes
	Steamed................	45 minutes
	Baked....................	60 minutes
Tomatoes	Boiled....................	5-15 minutes
Turnips	Boiled....................	25-40 minutes

BUYING GUIDE
Fresh Vegetables and Fruits

Experience is the best teacher in choosing quality, but here are a few pointers on buying some of the fruits and vegetables.

Asparagus: Stalks should be tender and firm, tips should be close and compact. Choose the stalks with very little white—they are more tender. Use asparagus soon—it toughens rapidly.

Beans, Snap: Those with small seeds inside the pods are best. Avoid beans with dry-looking pods.

Berries: Select plump, solid berries with good color. Avoid stained containers, indicating wet or leaky berries. Berries such as blackberries and raspberries with clinging caps may be under-ripe. Strawberries without caps may be too ripe.

Broccoli, Brussel Sprouts, and Cauliflower: Flower clusters on broccoli and cauliflower should be tight and close together. Brussel sprouts should be firm and compact. Smudgy, dirty spots may indicate insects.

Cabbage and Head Lettuce: Choose heads heavy for size. Avoid cabbage with worm holes, lettuce with discoloration or soft rot.

Cucumbers: Choose long, slender cucumbers for best quality. May be dark or medium green but yellowed ones are undesirable.

Melons: In cantaloupes, thick close netting on the rind indicates best quality. Cantaloupes are ripe when the stem scar is smooth and space between the netting is yellow or yellow-green. They are best when fully ripe with fruity odor.

Honeydews are ripe when rind has creamy to yellowish color and velvety texture. Immature honeydews are whitish-green.

Ripe watermelons have some yellow color on one side. If melons are white or pale green on one side, they are not ripe.

Oranges, Grapefruit, and Lemons: Choose those heavy for their size. Smoother, thinner skins usually indicate more juice. Most skin markings do not affect quality. Oranges with a slight greenish tinge may be just as ripe as fully colored ones. Light or greenish-yellow lemons are more tart than deep yellow ones. Avoid citrus fruits showing withered, sunken, or soft areas.

Peas and Lima Beans: Select pods that are well-filled but not bulging. Avoid dried, spotted, yellowed, or flabby pods.

TABLE FOR DRIED FRUITS		
Fruit	**Cooking Time**	**Amount of Sugar or Honey**
Apricots	About 40 minutes	1/4 c. for each cup of fruit
Figs	About 30 minutes	1 T. for each cup of fruit
Peaches	About 45 minutes	1/4 c. for each cup of fruit
Prunes	About 45 minutes	2 T. for each cup of fruit

BAKING PERFECT BREADS

Proportions

Biscuits ....To 1 c. flour use 1 1/4 tsp. Baking Powder
Muffins ....To 1 c. flour use 1 1/2 tsp. Baking Powder
Popovers...To 1 c. flour use 1 1/4 tsp. Baking Powder
Waffles ....To 1 c. flour use 1 1/4 tsp. Baking Powder
Cake with oil...To 1 c. flour use 1 tsp. Baking Powder

Rules for Use of Leavening Agents

1. To 1 teaspoon soda use 2 1/4 teaspoons cream of tartar, or 2 cups freshly soured milk, or 1 cup molasses.
2. In simple flour mixtures, use 2 teaspoons baking powder to leaven 1 cup flour. Reduce this amount 1/2 teaspoon for each egg used.
3. To substitute soda and an acid for baking powder, divide the amount of baking powder by 4. Take that as your measure of and add the acid according to rule 1 above.

Proportions for Batters and Dough

Pour Batter ....To 1 cup liquid use 1 cup flour
Drop Batter.............................To 1 cup liquid use 2 to 2 1/2 cups flour
Soft Dough ....To 1 cup liquid use 3 to 3 1/2 cups flour
Stiff Dough ....To 1 cup liquid use 4 cups flour

Hints for Baking Breads

Kneading the dough for a half minute after mixing improves the texture of baking powder biscuits.

Use cooking or salad oil in waffles and hot cakes in the place of shortening. No extra pan or bowl to melt the shortening and no waiting.

When bread is baking, a small dish of water in the oven will help to keep the crust from getting hard.

Dip the spoon in hot water to measure shortening, butter, etc., the fat will slip out more easily.

Small amounts of leftover corn may be added to pancake batter for variety.

To make bread crumbs, use fine cutter of the food grinder and tie a large paper bag over the spout to prevent flying crumbs.

When you are doing any sort of baking, you get better results if you remember to pre-heat your cookie sheet, muffin tins, or cake pans.

Oven Temperature Chart

Breads	Minutes	Temperature
Loaf	45 - 60	350° - 400°
Rolls	15 - 30	350° - 425°
Biscuits	10 - 15	400° - 450°
Muffins	15 - 25	400° - 425°
Cornbread	20 - 25	400° - 425°
Nut Bread	60 - 75	350°
Gingerbread	35 - 50	350° - 375°

BAKING PERFECT DESSERTS

For Perfect Cookies

Cookie dough that is to be rolled is much easier to handle after it has been refrigerated for 10 to 30 minutes. This keeps the dough from sticking, even though it may be soft. If not done, the soft dough may require more flour and too much flour makes cookies hard and brittle. In rolling, take out on a floured board, only as much dough as can be easily managed. Flour the rolling pin slightly and roll lightly to desired thickness. Cut shapes close together and keep all trimmings for the last roll. Place pans or sheets in upper third of oven. Watch cookies carefully while baking to avoid burning edges. When sprinkling sugar on cookies, try putting it into a salt shaker. It saves time.

For Perfect Pies and Cakes

❧ A pie crust will be more easily made and better if all the ingredients are cool.

❧ The lower crust should be placed in the pan so that it covers the surface smoothly. Be sure no air lurks beneath the surface, for it will push the crust out of shape in baking.

❧ Folding the top crust over the lower crust before crimping will keep the juices in the pie.

❧ In making custard type pies, bake at a high temperature for about ten minutes to prevent a soggy crust. Then finish baking at a low temperature.

❧ Fill cake pans about 2/3 full and spread batter well into corners and to the sides, leaving a slight hollow in the center.

❧ The cake is done when it shrinks from the sides of the pan or if it springs back when touched lightly with the finger.

❧ After a cake comes from the oven, it should be placed on a rack for about five minutes. Then the sides should be loosened and the cake turned out on a rack to finish cooling.

❧ Cakes should not be frosted until thoroughly cool.

❧ To prevent crust from becoming soggy with cream pie, sprinkle crust with powdered sugar.

Temperature Chart		
Food	**Temperature**	**Time**
Butter Cake, loaf	300° - 350°	50 - 80 min.
Butter Cake, layer	350° - 375°	25 - 35 min.
Cake, angel	350° - 375°	35 - 50 min.
Cake, sponge	350° - 375°	12 - 40 min.
Cake, fruit	250° - 275°	3 - 4 hours
Cookies, rolled	375° - 400°	6 - 12 min.
Cookies, drop	350° - 400°	8 - 15 min.
Cream Puffs	300° - 350°	45 - 60 min.
Meringue	300° - 350°	12 - 15 min.
Pie Crust (shell)	400° - 450°	10 - 12 min.

Food Quantities for Serving 25, 50, and 100 People

Food	25 Servings	50 Servings	100 Servings
Sandwiches:			
Bread	50 slices or 3 (1-lb.) loaves	100 slices or 6 (1-lb.) loaves	200 slices or 12 (1-lb.) loaves
Butter	1/2 pound	3/4 to 1 pound	1 1/2 pounds
Mayonnaise	1 cup	2 to 3 cups	4 to 6 cups
Mixed Filling (meat, eggs, fish)	1 1/2 quarts	2 1/2 to 3 quarts	5 to 6 quarts
Mixed Filling (sweet-fruit)	1 quart	1 3/4 to 2 quarts	2 1/2 to 4 quarts
Lettuce	1 1/2 heads	2 1/2 to 3 heads	5 to 6 heads
Meat, Poultry, or Fish:			
Hot dogs (beef)	6 1/2 pounds	13 pounds	25 pounds
Hamburger	9 pounds	18 pounds	35 pounds
Turkey or Chicken	13 pounds	25 to 35 pounds	50 to 75 pounds
Fish, large whole (round)	13 pounds	25 pounds	50 pounds
Fish fillets or steak	7 1/2 pounds	15 pounds	30 pounds
Salads, Casseroles:			
Potato Salad	4 1/4 quarts	1 1/4 gallons	4 1/4 gallons
Scalloped Potatoes	4 1/2 quarts or 1 12" x 20" pan	8 1/2 quarts	17 quarts
Spaghetti	1 1/4 gallons	2 1/2 gallons	5 gallons
Baked Beans	3/4 gallon	1 1/4 gallons	2 1/2 gallons
Jello Salad	3/4 gallon	1 1/4 gallons	2 1/2 gallons
Ice Cream:			
Brick	3 1/4 quarts	6 1/2 quarts	12 1/2 quarts
Bulk	2 1/4 quarts	4 1/2 quarts or 1 1/4 gallons	9 quarts or 2 1/2 gallons
Beverages:			
Coffee	1/2 pound and 1 1/2 gal. water	1 pound and 3 gal. water	2 pounds and 6 gal. water
Tea	1/12 pound and 1 1/2 gal. water	1/6 pound 3 gal. water	1/3 pound and 6 gal. water
Lemonade	10 to 15 lemons, 1 1/2 gal. water	20 to 30 lemons, 3 gal. water	40 to 60 lemons, 6 gal. water
Desserts:			
Watermelon	37 1/2 pounds	75 pounds	150 pounds
Cake	1 10" x 12" sheet cake	1 12" x 20" sheet cakes	2 12" x 20" sheet cakes
	2 8" layer cakes	3 10" layer cakes	6 10" layer cakes
Whipping Cream	1 pint	1 quart	2 quarts

EQUIVALENCY CHART

FOOD	QUANTITY	YIELD
unsifted flour	3 3/4 cups	1 pound
sifted flour	4 cups	1 pound
sifted cake flour	4 1/2 cups	1 pound
rye flour	5 cups	1 pound
flour	1 pound	4 cups
baking powder	5 1/2 ounces	1 cup
cornmeal	3 cups	1 pound
cornstarch	3 cups	1 pound
lemon	1 medium	3 tablespoons juice
apple	1 medium	1 cup
orange	3-4 medium	1 cup juice
onion	1 medium	1/2 cup
unshelled walnuts	1 pound	1 1/2 to 1 3/4 cups
sugar	2 cups	1 pound
powdered sugar	3 1/2 cups	1 pound
brown sugar	2 1/2 cups	1 pound
spaghetti	7 ounces	4 cups cooked
noodles (uncooked)	4 ounces (1 1/2 - 2 cups)	2-3 cups cooked
macaroni (uncooked)	4 ounces (1 1/4 cups)	2 1/4 cups cooked
macaroni (cooked)	6 cups	8-ounce package
noodles (cooked)	7 cups	8-ounce package
long-grain rice (uncooked)	1 cup	3-4 cups cooked
saltine crackers	28 crackers	1 cup fine crumbs
butter	1 stick or 1/4 lb.	1/2 cup
cocoa	4 cups	1 pound
chocolate (bitter)	1 ounce	1 square
coconut	2 2/3 cups	1 1/2 pound carton
marshmallows	16	1/4 pound
graham crackers	14 squares	1 cup fine crumbs
vanilla wafers	22	1 cup fine crumbs
bread	1 1/2 slices	1 cup soft crumbs
bread	1 slice	1/4 cup fine, dry crumbs
egg whites	8-10	1 cup
egg yolks	10-12	1 cup
egg	4-5 whole	1 cup
flavored gelatin	3 1/4 ounces	1/2 cup
unflavored gelatin	1/4 ounce	1 tablespoon
nuts (chopped)	1 cup	1/4 pound
almonds	3 1/2 cups	1 pound
walnuts (broken)	3 cups	1 pound
raisins	1 pound	3 1/2 cups
rice	2 1/3 cups	1 pound
American cheese (grated)	5 cups	1 pound
American cheese (cubed)	2 2/3 cups	1 pound
cream cheese	6 2/3 tablespoons	3-ounce package
zwieback (crumbled)	4	1 cup
banana (mashed)	1 medium	1/3 cup
coffee (ground)	5 cups	1 pound
evaporated milk	1 cup	3 cups whipped

TERMS USED IN COOKING

Au gratin: Topped with crumbs and/or cheese and browned in the oven or under the broiler.

Au jus: Served in its own juices.

Baste: To moisten foods during cooking with pan drippings or special sauce to add flavor and prevent drying.

Bisque: A thick cream soup.

Blanch: To immerse in rapidly boiling water and allow to cook slightly.

Cream: To soften a fat, especially butter, by beating it at room temperature. Butter and sugar are often creamed together, making a smooth, soft paste.

Crimp: To seal the edges of a two-crust pie either by pinching them at intervals with the fingers or by pressing them together with the tines of a fork.

Crudites: An assortment of raw vegetables, i.e. carrots, broccoli, mushrooms, served as an hors d'oeuvre often accompanied by a dip.

Degrease: To remove fat from the surface of stews, soups, or stock. Usually cooled in the refrigerator, so that fat hardens and is easily removed.

Dredge: To coat lightly with flour, cornmeal, etc.

Entree: The main course.

Fold: To incorporate a delicate substance, such as whipped cream or beaten egg whites, into another substance without releasing air bubbles. A spatula is used to gently bring part of the mixture from the bottom of the bowl to the top. The process is repeated, while slowly rotating the bowl, until the ingredients are thoroughly blended.

Glaze: To cover with a glossy coating, such as a melted and somewhat diluted jelly for fruit desserts.

Julienne: To cut vegetables, fruits, or cheeses into match-shaped slivers.

Marinade: To allow food to stand in a liquid to tenderize or to add flavor.

Meuniere: Dredged with flour and sauteed in butter.

Mince: To chop or cut food into very small pieces.

Parboil: To boil until partially cooked; to blanch. Usually this procedure is followed by final cooking in a seasoned sauce.

Pare: To remove the outermost skin of a fruit or vegetable.

Poach: To cook very gently in hot liquid kept just below the boiling point.

Puree: To mash foods until perfectly smooth by hand, by rubbing through a sieve or food mill, or by whirling in a blender or food processor.

Refresh: To run cold water over food that has been parboiled, to stop the cooking process quickly.

Saute: To cook and/or brown food in a small quantity of hot oil.

Scald: To heat to just below the boiling point, when tiny bubbles appear at the edge of the saucepan.

Simmer: To cook in liquid just below the boiling point. The surface of the liquid should be barely moving, broken from time to time by slowly rising bubbles.

Steep: To let food stand in (hot) liquid to extract or to enhance flavor, like tea in hot water or poached fruits in sugar syrup.

Toss: To combine ingredients with a lifting motion.

Whip: To beat rapidly to incorporate air and produce expansion, as in heavy cream or egg whites.

Hints

The following ingredients can be found in Indian grocery or Asian food stores. Red lentils, unsweetened desiccated coconut, Biryani paste, canned jackfruit, lemongrass, cardamon pods, dry chili peppers, cinnamon sticks, whole cloves, coriander seeds, green chili peppers, Basmati rice, coconut milk and cashews.

Most ingredients can be bought from health food stores.

Some big supermarkets have an Asian food section. Mangoes, when ripe, are slightly red in color and soft to the touch. It can be purchased at Asian Food Stores or any supermarket.

It is best to use Japanese eggplant for curry dishes. Japanese eggplant available in Asian food stores only.

Store dry herbs and spices in an airtight container.

Buy fresh herbs in small quantities.

Substitute black pepper, limejuice and salt instead of lemon pepper.

Spices give flavor and color to cooking. Turmeric is used to make curries yellow. Chili powder and paprika make curries red. Roasted curry powder makes curries brown. Cayenne pepper makes curries red and hot.

Vegetable Lamprais parcels, page 123, can be made and frozen. Thaw in refrigerator. Follow as instructed on page 123.

Order a book for a friend...

It's a Perfect Gift!

ORDER FORM

For additional copies of this cookbook contact:

Trafford Publishing, 6E–2333 Government St.,
Victoria, BC v8t 4p4 CANADA
phone 250 383 6864 (toll-free 1 888 232 4444)
fax 250 383 6804; email to orders@trafford.com

Please mail me _____ copies of your Easy Vegetarian
Cooking With Herbs and Spices at $26.95 each $_____

Applicable taxes $_____

Shipping and handling $_____
(please contact Trafford Publishing for quote)

Enclosed is my check or money order for $_____

Mail books to:

    Name: _____

    Address: _____

    City: _____ State _____ Zip _____

ISBN 141207337-5

Printed in the United States
By Bookmasters